Money Sense

Money Sense

A YOUNG PERSON'S GUIDE TO FINANCIAL FREEDOM

ED MURPHY

Wrightbooks

First published in 2001 by Wrightbooks.

Wrightbooks Pty Ltd
PO Box 270
Elsternwick
Victoria 3185

Ph: (03) 9532 7082
Fax: (03) 9532 7084
E-mail: info@wrightbooks.com.au
Website: www.wrightbooks.com.au

National Library of Australia Cataloguing-in-publication data:

Murphy, Ed.
Money sense: a young person's guide to financial freedom.

Includes index.
ISBN 1 876627 51 4.

1. Youth - Finance, Personal. I. Title.

640.42

Cover design by Rob Cowpe
Illustrations by Mairead Murphy
Printed in Australia by McPherson's Printing Group
ISBN 1 876627 51 4

The author and publisher would like to thank *The Australian* for allowing the use of their sharemarket table in Chapter 9.

NOTE

Contents

For Ben, Mairead and Caitlin

Preface

Once upon a time there was a popular song that asked "Who wants to be a millionaire?" Of course it then went on to answer its own question: "I do!" More recently the words have been used as the title for a popular TV quiz show. Again the answer to the question is "we all do!"

It may surprise many people to know that more than a million dollars will pass through their fingers in the course of a working lifetime—but very few of us will become millionaires. One of the reasons most Australians do not end up wealthy is that they do not understand how money works in their lives. At school they acquired the knowledge and skills needed to earn money. Their family and the media have taught them how to spend money. There seems to be no place for most people to learn how to keep and grow money.

This book sets out to demystify the process of managing your money. It is written in a way that ordinary people will understand. It is not written for accountants, for financial planners or for share brokers. It is written for beginners—whether they are teenagers who have just begun to earn money in a part-time job, or middle-aged people who have begun to think about their financial future.

Money Sense is divided into two parts. The first will help you understand the language of finance and the need to start accumulating wealth as early as possible in your life. The second part deals with investment choices—how you can grow the wealth you have accumulated by saving.

Money Sense is a 'big picture' book about wealth creation. It gives you an overview that is needed to make sense of all the details. It begins from a simple premise—life is about choice. *Money Sense* will tell you about your choices, and their consequences. What you do about it will then be up to you. I hope that learning about the choices you have will be an interesting and liberating experience for you.

Ed Murphy
Ballarat
January 2001

Part One

How to Become Wealthy

Chapter 1

The Dream

Every week in Australia millions of people spend millions of dollars on lotto, gambling or raffles. The vast majority of them don't win, but they will be back next week to pursue the dream of huge wealth. Why do they do it?

A television ad for Tattslotto offers one answer. In the advertisement a middle-aged mother is working in a crowded kitchen, surrounded by husband, children, granny and the dog. She asks for quiet while the lotto results appear on the television on top of the fridge. As each number appears she glances at the ticket she holds tightly in her hand, and her eyes open wider. Finally she lets out a whoop of joy. She won!

The slogan for the advertisement is "Come on George, Tatts me out of here". This taps into the dream of many Australians, that they will get "out of here"; get out of a life where bills are a worry, where luxuries are few and where the future is uncertain. When lotto winners are interviewed after their big win, the interviewer always asks what they intend to do with their new-found wealth. The replies are remarkably consistent; pay off the mortgage, have a holiday, stop work, help family members.

For most lotto winners, money is not an end in itself, it is a means to do things that they have only dreamed about until now—to be financially secure, to purchase some luxuries, to leave a job they dislike and to help others. These are all wonderful goals and most of us would share them.

But are these goals only attainable by the lucky few lotto winners?

This book will help you understand money in a way that will enable you to make profitable choices in your life. Perhaps you can use this information to *work* your way into the position of a lotto winner without having to rely on luck.

Who Wants to be a Millionaire?

Think for a moment about a simple calculation. If the average Australian wage is $37,000 per year, and an average worker spends 45 years (age 20 to age 65) in the workforce, how much will that person earn in a working lifetime?

Does it surprise you to learn that an average person will have almost $1.67 million pass through their fingers in a working lifetime? This is the *average* worker—a large proportion of the workforce is above the average, so we should be bumping into millionaires on every street corner. But you can probably think of many reasons why most Australians spend their money and never become wealthy. One of the reasons is our perception of time.

Our Perception of Time

One reason many of us do not become wealthy is because we do not *aim* to be. To understand why so many Australians *wish* they were rich but never get around to doing anything about it, we have to understand how we see time.

Time is a curious thing. Some cultures tend to see time as a circle, where birth – life – death – rebirth, etc. go on continuously.

In Western culture we generally have a linear view of time. The past – present – future are arranged in a straight line.

If you had to draw a timeline representing recent history, it could be divided into equal-sized segments representing the decades, with important events placed at the correct location along the line. For example, a twentieth-century timeline would be divided into ten equal parts, with the first part representing the time from 1900 to 1910, the second 1910 to 1920, and so on. World War I would then be marked in the second decade between 1914 and 1918. The Great Depression would be marked in the third and fourth decades between 1929 and 1934, and you could add in other events as well. Your birth-date might be closer to the end of the timeline. It might end up looking like Figure 1.1.

We know in theory that the ten years of the 1920s was as long as the ten years of the 1990s, but our mind does a curious thing to time. It places more significance on time closer to the present and less significance on time far away from the present. It does this simply because we can envision what might happen in the near future much more than we can guess

Figure 1.1
TIMELINE

what might happen in the distant future. This peculiar mind trick has a profound effect on the way we view our lives. For example, a secondary-school student aged 15 might see the stages of his or her life in the following distorted way (with the larger figures showing what are perceived to be the 'more important' ages):

0.....5...... **10**....... **15**........**20**.......25.....30...35...40...45...50...60...70...80...90

So, even though we know that every decade in our life is as long as every other decade, we are much more aware of the present and near future than we are of the distant future. In fact, the more distant the future, the less significance we tend to place on it.

As a result of our mind distorting our perception of time we tend to:

- Be more concerned about the present rather than the future.
- Procrastinate (put off doing things until later).
- Drift along without long-term goals.

The Reality of Time

Obviously each one of us lives a unique life, and we cannot foretell the future. However, by using a bit of imagination it is possible to sketch a general picture for you to think about.

For You To Do...

Find a piece of paper and a pen and draw a timeline similar to the one on the previous page. Divide the line into decades of equal length, starting from your birth at year 0 through to age 90. On your timeline mark in the events listed opposite. Some will be in your past, the rest may or may not be in your future. If you do not think a

particular event is going to occur in your own life, put it in anyway just for this exercise.

Stage	*Event*
1.	Start school
2.	Start secondary school
3.	End secondary school
4.	Post-school training/education
5.	First full-time job
6.	Marriage
7.	First child
8.	One parent leaves workforce to raise children, causing a drop in family income
9.	Second child
10.	Child-rearing parent returns to workforce
11.	First child leaves home
12.	Second child leaves home
13.	Retirement from workforce
14.	Death

From your timeline calculate the following:

1. The number of years your parents spent supporting you before your independence (Stages 1 to 5).

2. The number of years you will be an independent, income-producing adult, before you begin to support your own children (Stages 5 to 7).

3. The number of years you will spend supporting others, from the birth of your first child to the independence of your second child (Stages 7 to 12).

4. The number of years between the independence of your second child and your retirement from the workforce (Stages 12 to 13).
5. The number of retirement years you will live without an income from paid employment (Stage 13 until death).

Now answer the following questions:

1. Why is the length of Stage 5 to 6 important to your financial well-being?
2. Why is the length of Stage 12 to 13 important financially?
3. How will you survive financially without a job in Stage 13 until death?

At present you may have some hazy answers to these questions. As you work through the following chapters you will be able to clarify these. As you gain a clearer understanding of the financial realities of life you may choose to plan and set long-term goals.

The decision is yours. Will you work towards the dream or will you still be saying "tatts me out of here" in 30 years time?

Chapter Summary

- You can *work* your way into the position of a lotto winner without having to rely on luck.
- An average person will have almost $1.67 million pass through their fingers in a working lifetime.
- One reason many of us do not become wealthy is because we do not *aim* to be.

Chapter 2

Money Language, Money Facts

When people discuss cricket it is difficult if they do not have a common language and an understanding of the terms used in cricket. For instance, imagine how hard it would be to discuss a cricket match with a friend who did not know the meaning of the terms wicket, spinner, LBW, six, four, bye, wicket keeper and slips.

Some people struggle financially because they do not understand the language of money. You might describe them as 'financially illiterate'. This chapter provides a lesson in financial language and some basic money facts, so that we can both speak the same language and you can understand later chapters in the book more easily.

What is Money?

Once upon a time people exchanged goods as a way of paying for things. You work for me for a day and I will pay you a bag of corn. Or, you give me that belt and I will give you three cabbages. This system of exchanging goods and services is known as 'barter'. In simple communities it works very well.

But what if you wanted to travel to get something far away from home? It might be inconvenient to carry a load of cabbages to pay for things. So societies invented symbols for the cabbages. These symbols might be sea shells or silver and gold; all that was needed was for people to agree that the symbols had a certain value.

In time trading became bigger and more complex. Sometimes it was inconvenient or unsafe to carry around the load of gold needed to pay for very big items. In these situations people invented a piece of paper which promised to pay a certain amount of gold to the bearer when he or she produced the promise. Paper money was born.

Essentially, the money we carry around or hand over at the supermarket checkout is a promise to the receiver that goods or services matching the value of the note can be redeemed by him or her. As long as everyone accepts that an oblong blue piece of plastic represents $10 worth of goods, we don't actually have to carry around mountains of cabbages or corn, or even gold.

This promise is backed by the government of the country issuing the notes. As long as everyone is confident that the society can supply the required amount of cabbages whenever someone presents an oblong piece of blue plastic, all is well. If the economy of the country is not going well, and there is some doubt that it can keep its promise to supply $10 worth of cabbages on demand, the value of the oblong blue plastic declines. This is why you might have heard on the news that the value of the Australian dollar has gone up or down on a particular day.

To sum up, money is a symbol that represents a certain value. It is a promise to supply to the bearer a certain value of goods and/or services. However, the value of the symbol and the value of the goods and services can change with time.

Interest

Imagine you own a house that you don't need to live in yourself. You may decide to allow someone else to live in it. Of course you would charge rent for the use of your house.

If you transfer this situation to money you will understand the meaning of interest. If I have money and you would like to use it—to buy a car, to start a business, to go on a holiday—you can rent my money for a while. Of course, like the tenant, you will have to return the house (the money) as well as pay the rent (the interest).

You have probably been involved in renting money for some time. When you put your money into a bank account, you are actually renting it to the bank. The transaction looks something like this:

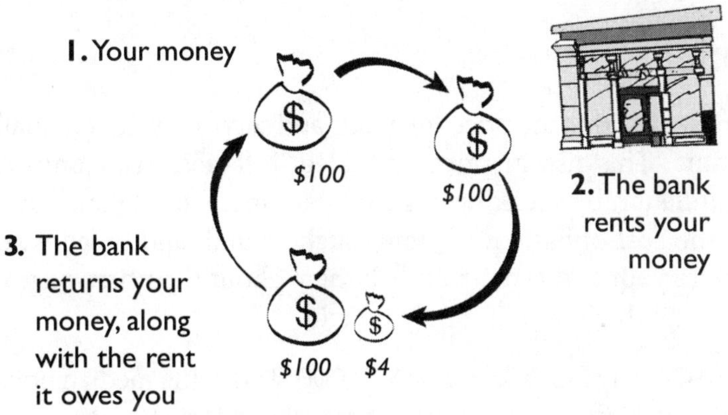

If the bank owned the money and you wanted to rent it for a while it would be called taking out a loan. The transaction would look like this:

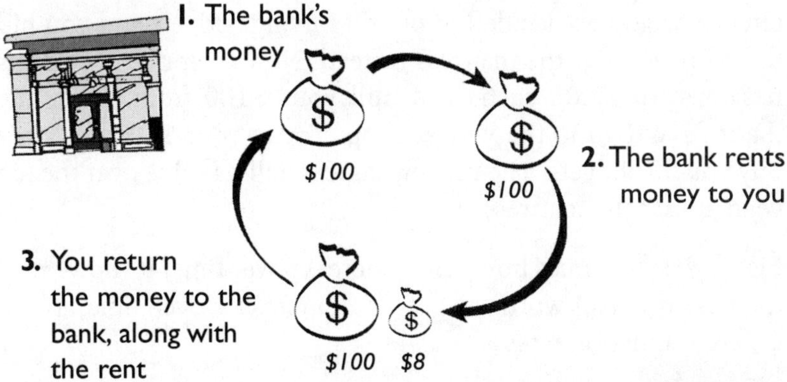

The difference in the 'rent' the bank pays the depositors compared to the 'rent' it charges on loans is a source of profit for the bank. If you want to get involved in the renting of money then you will obviously try to:

- Charge the highest 'rent' possible for your money (i.e. find a bank account paying the highest amount of interest).
- Pay the lowest 'rent' possible for the use of someone else's money (i.e. take out a loan with the lowest interest rate).

Inflation

Generally speaking the prices of goods and services go up gradually over time. This rise in prices is called 'inflation'. You find out about inflation by speaking with an older member of your family about the cost of basic food items such as milk and bread when they were young. Alternatively ask them about their first wage or the price of the first house they bought.

In the 1970s my first house cost $29,000. Today the median house price in the Melbourne suburb where I lived is $210,000.

The flip-side of the coin when it comes to rising prices is that money is falling in value. Assume you had $100 ten years ago, and if you went to your local widget shop you could have bought 100 widgets because widgets were $1.00 each back then. However, ten years ago you decided to put off buying widgets and you hid the money under the mattress instead. Now the price of widgets has risen to $2.00 each. You pull your $100 from under the mattress and go to the widget shop. Today your $100 will only buy you 50 widgets. The money has lost half its value over the ten years under the mattress.

Figure 2.1 illustrates how prices increase over time. It shows how the cost of $100 worth of groceries increases over time at two different inflation rates.

Figure 2.1 **INFLATION**

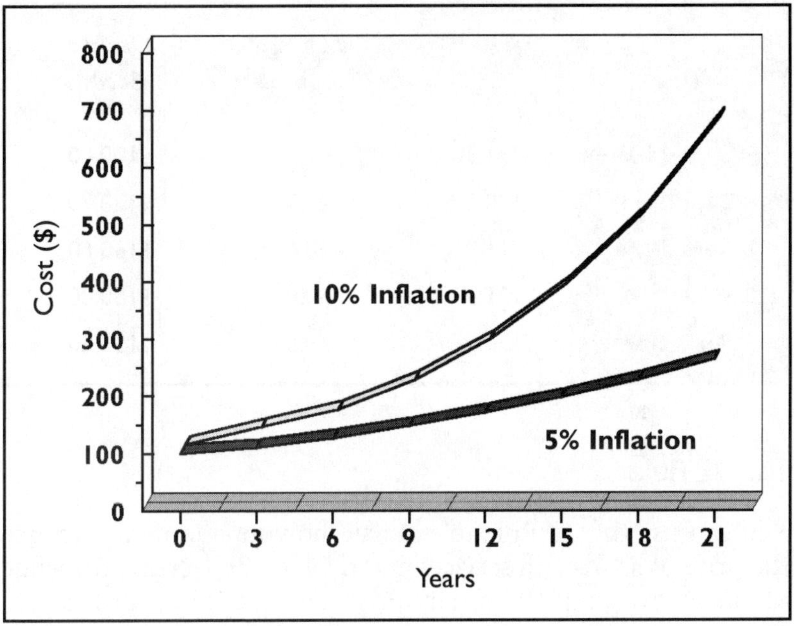

So inflation means that prices rise and the value of money falls. Anyone who puts money under the mattress will find that it gradually loses value with every passing year.

The Consumer Price Index (CPI) is the government's way of measuring price increases in a selection of goods and services that represent the spending of the average family. If the CPI rose annually by 5% it means that what you could buy for $100 last year will now cost you $105. The flip side is that the $100 placed under the mattress last year will now only buy goods and services that were worth about $95 when you put the money under the mattress. You therefore have to think of something better to do with your money than hide it under the mattress!

The CPI gives us an easy way to see the movement in prices over several years. It was set at 100 in late 1989. The table on the following page shows how prices have risen since September 1985.

Table 2.1 **CPI MOVEMENT**

Date	*CPI*	*CPI Change Since Sept. '85*	*Cost of Goods*
Sept 1985	71.3	–	$100.00
Sept 1989	100.0	28.7	$128.70
Sept 1996	111.9	40.6	$140.60
Sept 1998	121.3	50.0	$150.00
Sept 2000	130.9	59.6	$159.60

The 72 Rule

You can use the 72 Rule to estimate how inflation will increase the price of goods and services and how it will decrease the value of money over time. It's so simple you can do it in your head.

Rise in Prices

If you know the current inflation rate, divide this figure into 72. Your answer will be the number of years it will take prices to double.

For example, if inflation is currently running at 6%, divide 72 by 6, which equals 12. Prices will therefore double every 12 years.

Drop in the Value of the Dollar

If the current inflation rate is 6%, divide 72 by 6, which equals 12. The dollar will halve in value every 12 years. If the inflation rate rose to 8%, money would halve in value in 9 years (72 ÷ 8 = 9).

If you understand about inflation you will make sure that any money you have will be growing at a percentage rate higher than inflation. If it is not growing faster than inflation the numbers may be going up but the value is slipping away. You can see this in the following example.

Suppose you had $100 to put in the bank for a year. The bank will pay you 3% interest so that at the end of the year you will have $103 ($100.00 + $3.00 = $103.00). But if the inflation rate is 5%, the price of $100 worth of goods and services will have risen to $105 at the end of the year. Your $103 at the end of the year will not buy the same amount of goods and services that it did at the beginning—your money has actually gone down *in value*, even though the *numbers* have gone *up* ($100 to $103).

Taxes

There is an old saying that there are only two things in life that are certain—death and taxes. Not many people enjoy paying tax, but we have to be realistic about it. If we want an army and police force to protect us, a court system to ensure justice, roads to drive on, hospitals to care for us when we are ill and schools to educate children we have to pay for these services. American Supreme Court Justice Oliver Wendall Holmes summed it up when he said "Taxes are the price we pay for a civil society."

All levels of government collect taxes from citizens so that they can provide services. Your local council needs the money raised from property rates to pay for roads, parks and garbage collection. Your State Government puts taxes on items such as petrol, tobacco and alcohol in order to pay for police, education and hospitals. The Federal Government collects taxes to pay for the armed forces, education, major highways and the costs of running the country.

Types of Tax

It is worth having an understanding of the three main types of Federal Government taxes because they will have an impact on your ability to become wealthy. They are:

1. **Goods and Services Tax (GST):** This is a 10% tax on most goods and services that we purchase. Items such as some types of food, medical expenses, education expenses and residential rents are exempt so that the tax does not hit the poorer members of the community too heavily.

2. **Capital Gains Tax (CGT):** A tax charged on any gains you make from assets that have risen in value by the time you sell them. This can include investments in the stock market and investments in property. The house you live in is exempt.
3. **Income tax:** As the name suggests, this is a tax on the income you make from any source. Workers will find that their employer has already deducted tax from their pay packet. However, there are other sources of income. If your generous great-grandmother left you a fortune in her will, the money may be sitting in a bank account earning you interest, or it may be invested on the stock market earning you dividends (part of the company profits). These sources are also classed as income and they are taxed.

Why should you be concerned about taxes? Firstly, this will help you to calculate your income—all you really have is what is left over after tax has been taken out (your net income). Secondly, it will help you to understand the full cost of an item that is paid for in after-tax dollars. Thirdly, it will help you to arrange your affairs so that you do not pay more than your fair share of tax.

How Tax is Calculated

The different types of taxes are calculated in the following ways:

1. The GST is charged automatically by the provider of most goods and services at a rate of one-eleventh of the price of the item. This is another way of saying that one-tenth of the price is added on to the base price. There are exceptions, as mentioned earlier. As a broad generalisation, you will not be charged GST on some foods, medical services or education expenses. However, there are many cases where the GST will be charged in these areas—for instance on take-away foods, on medical goods such as bandages and on school books.

2. Capital gains include all increases in the value of any investments you sell, whether this is land, buildings or shares. Capital Gains Tax is generally calculated on *half* of this gain in value. For instance if you bought some shares for $5,000 and later sold them for $6,800 you have a capital gain of: $6,800 – $5,000 = $1,800. Only half of this will be taxed, so you will have to calculate tax on $900. This $900 will be taxed at your marginal rate, which is the highest rate of tax you are currently paying on your income (see following page). In the chapters on investment you will find out more about income and capital gain.
3. Income tax is the most confusing to calculate for most people. The income tax scale has been designed to take progressively larger bites out of your income dollars as your income increases. This makes it a 'progressive' tax, hitting the rich more than the poor.

Figure 2.2 (overleaf) illustrates how income tax increases as income grows. For the first $6,000 you earn, there is no tax at all. The figure of $6,000 is known as the 'tax-free threshold' for this reason. Every dollar you earn above $6,000 will be taxed at 17¢ in the dollar, up to $20,000. So, if your total earnings for the year were $6,002, you would have to pay 34¢ (17¢ × 2) in income tax. If your total earnings for the year were $6,005 you would have to pay 85¢ (17¢ × 5) income tax. This rate continues until you earn over $20,000. Once your income rises above $20,000 you will have to pay 30¢ in every dollar above $20,000 until your income reaches $50,000. Between $50,000 and $60,000 you will pay 42¢ in every dollar in tax and income above $60,000 will be taxed at a rate of 47¢ in each dollar. This is the highest tax rate.

Figure 2.3 (on page 19) shows how income tax is calculated on a number of different incomes. Notice that Bob pays no tax since his income does not exceed the tax-free threshold. Many teenagers with part-time jobs would be in the same situation as Bob. They should check whether their employer has taken any tax out of

Figure 2.2
INCOME TAX RATES

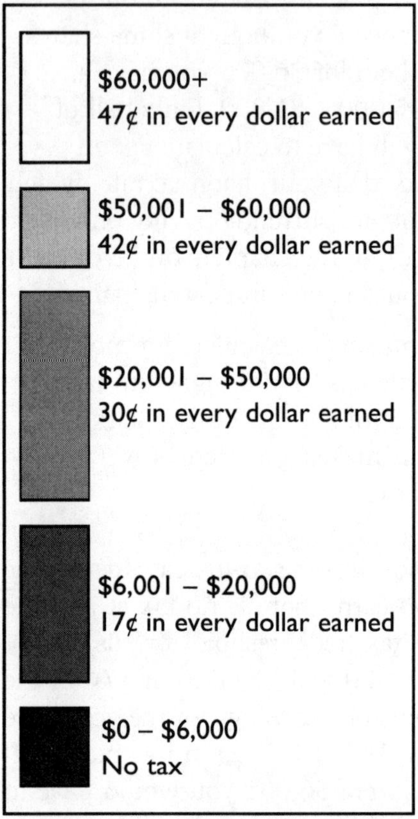

their wages to pay the government. If tax has been deducted by the employer—perhaps thinking the person would be working more hours—then he or she can ask the taxation department for a refund of the money incorrectly deducted from the wages.

The second thing you can see from Figure 2.3 is the progressive nature of income tax. Anthony is paying more tax on the highest portion of his earnings than Anna pays.

The rate of tax charged on the highest portion of a person's income is known as the 'marginal rate', and it is the rate used to calculate any Capital Gains Tax. So you can see, Anthony will pay more CGT as well as more income tax.

Chapter Summary

- The value of money is not fixed.
- You should look for the highest rate of interest (or returns) on your own money if you lend it to someone else, such as a bank.
- You should try to pay the least amount of interest possible if you use someone else's money.

(cont'd...)

Figure 2.3 INCOME TAX EXAMPLES

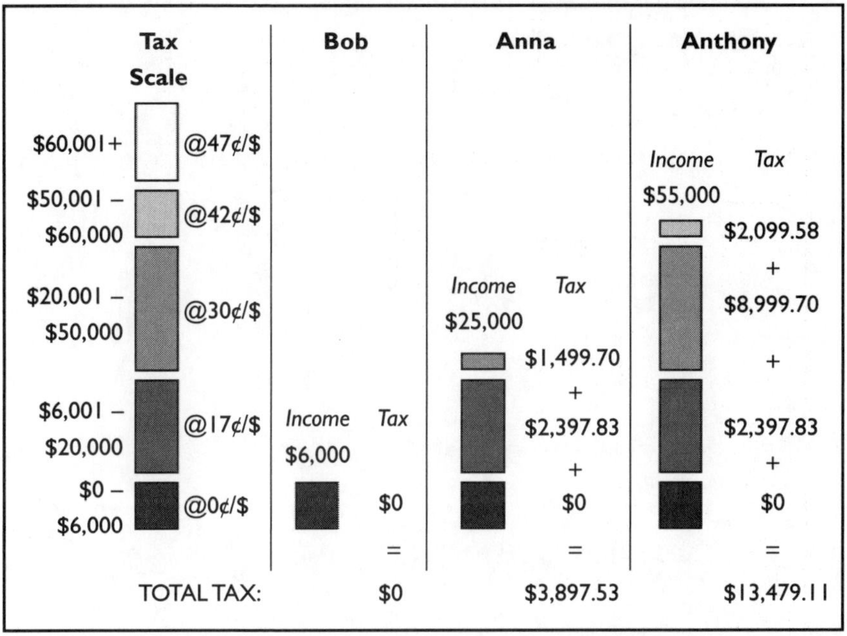

Note: A 1.5% Medicare levy is also paid by most taxpayers.
There are also rebates for low-income earners.

Chapter Summary (Cont'd)

- Rising prices (inflation) make your dollar worth less. So always ensure that your money is placed where it will grow in value faster than inflation is shrinking its value.
- Taxes are inevitable and necessary. Understanding the three ways the government taxes your wealth will help you to avoid paying more than your fair share, and allow you to calculate more accurately how much money you will have.

Chapter 3

Money Flows

The average weekly full-time wage in Australia is approximately $37,000. This figure is slightly misleading however because it is increased by a small number of workers in top management or professions who earn salaries in the hundreds of thousands, and in extreme cases, in the millions. A more accurate figure for the 'average' Australian would be the *median* income of about $34,000. The median is the figure where half of all wages are above and half of all wages are below.

Let's use the median figure for a moment. Over a 45-year working life (age 20 to age 65), this average worker will earn:

$34,000 x 45 = $1,530,000

This is an awful lot of money, and many of us would wonder where it all goes. Of course it would be unrealistic to expect this worker to earn his or her way to being a millionaire because he or she would have to pay for food, shelter, clothing and a multitude of other goods and services. To find out what really happens to the $1.53 million we have to follow the money flows.

The flow of money in most people's lives is shown below.

Figure 3.1 AVERAGE AUSTRALIAN'S MONEY FLOW

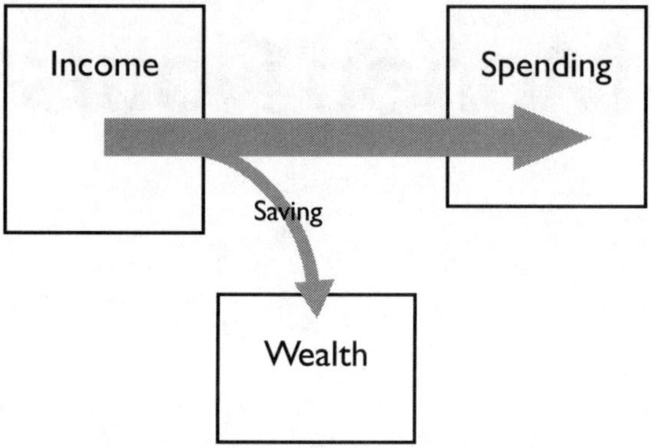

Spending is how you use that money to purchase goods or services. The *wealth* box is the important one. Your wealth is what you have managed to keep!

Most Australians have an income from employment of some sort. Most of this income flows out of their pockets towards regular living expenses, their spending—the groceries, transport, schooling costs, paying off the house or paying the rent, some entertainment, clothes, shoes, etc. You can see from the diagram that only a small amount of income is captured in the wealth box. For many Australians the wealth box will include their home and car. They divert some of their income into paying off these items because if they didn't the bank would evict them or the dealer would repossess their car.

Even teenagers have money flows. For a teenager, income might be pocket money or money from a part-time job. If you are a teenager still at school it may surprise you how much money has already flowed through your fingers.

Saving

We Australians are not great savers. Later you will learn how the government is trying to get us to change our ways by making saving into a superannuation scheme compulsory for most workers.

For many young people, saving is the furthest thing from their minds. They leave school and enter the bright new world of adulthood with more money in their pockets than they have ever had before. They are in the business of impressing others and enjoying their new-found freedom, so they spend up big on clothes, shoes, cosmetics, hair styles, entertainment, partying, cars and travel. You don't have to be Einstein to predict what their money flows will look like.

For You To Do...

Redraw Figure 3.1 and fill in your own money flow figures, then answer the following questions:

1. How much wealth do you have?
2. Where do you keep it?
3. How much interest is the bank giving you for the use of your wealth?
4. Check with your friends. Adjust for income differences (if your friend earns twice as much as you do, you should have half the wealth). After adjusting for income differences, how does your level of wealth compare with others? What are the reasons for any differences?
5. What is the critical factor influencing how wealthy you are?

Chapter Summary

- Many Australians will have one million dollars or more pass through their hands in a lifetime.
- Most of the money will be spent on things we need to survive (food, clothes, shelter) and things we like to have (recreation, holidays, toys).
- Our wealth is the part of our income that we manage to keep.

Chapter 4

Be Rich or Just Look Rich?

Our society was labelled a 'consumer society' as far back as the 1950s. Its main characteristic is an ever-rising level of consumption by the majority of people. Sometimes our grandparents tell us about their youth and we wonder at how simple and primitive it all was. We think this way because we have been conditioned to expect change and improvement and more of everything.

Television has played a significant part in this. Next time you are watching pay attention to the lifestyles of the families portrayed. Television families live in a house that most Australians would envy, they have new cars, their clothes are always stylish, they have holidays in exotic places, they regularly stay in hotels, they spend a lot of time relaxing and they never seem to be bothered with bills. We watch these people over countless hours and we begin to think of them as 'normal' people. The next little step is to believe that we must be like them in order to be 'normal' too.

Being normal isn't enough to satisfy us, though. Psychologist Abraham Maslow was intrigued about what made people do things, what motivated them. He suggested a theory of motivation which said that we humans are never satisfied.

Figure 4.1 MASLOW'S HIERARCHY OF NEEDS

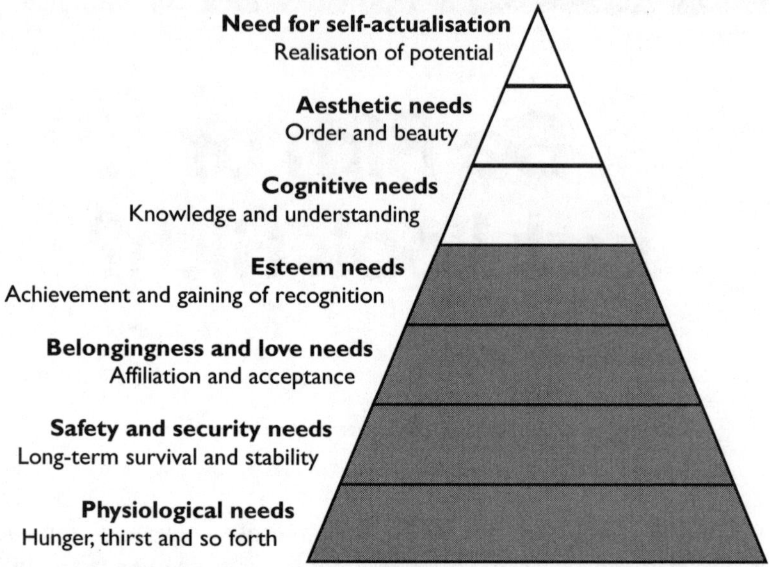

If we start with nothing we want our physical needs met, with food, clothing and shelter. But once we have sufficient food, clothing and shelter we don't then sit down and say "Now I have enough". We are driven to want more, and we turn our minds to gaining status and acceptance after we have all our food, clothing and shelter needs met. We need to be respected by our companions, we need to feel accepted and important.

These are deep needs in human beings, and wherever there is a deep need there is someone willing to exploit it. So along come a host of sellers, helped by their advertisers, to tell you that:

- You will have respect and success if you have their product.
- You will be accepted and looked up to if you drive their cars, wear their clothes or live in their houses.

It is at this point that you have to make a choice. Once your food, clothing and shelter needs have been met, where will the rest of your money go? Would you be happy to just *look rich* or would you prefer to actually *be rich*?

The *Look Rich* Option

Money flows are often a matter of choice. At this point many people decide they would prefer to *look rich* rather than *be rich*. The *look rich* choose to have most of their income flow through to the spending box, with very little, if any, of their income being diverted to the wealth box.

Figure 4.2 *LOOK RICH* MONEY FLOW

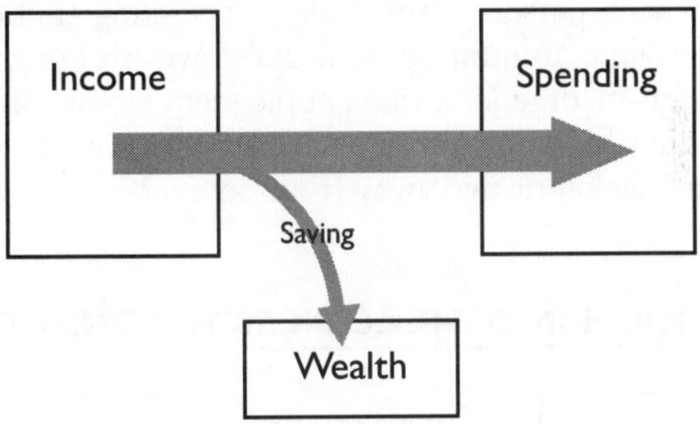

Look rich people find it very hard to become wealthy because of this. And to make things worse, they are caught on a treadmill that they cannot afford to step off. Their lifestyle of conspicuous consumption depends on a constant income flow. As soon as they stop working their income stops and they plunge into a much more restricted lifestyle (or even poverty).

The *look rich* get enjoyment out of their luxury cars, their large impressive house, their fashionable clothes and their expensive resort holidays. The driving force in their lives seems to be a desire for instant gratification as well as a need to impress those around them with how successful they are. Sometimes they will work very hard to gain the income to maintain this lifestyle. At the end of this lifetime of hard work, however, they may have little to show for all the effort apart from a grand house, lots of out-of-date clothes, a few second-hand cars and maybe a boat.

They have no savings and no way to generate income without employment. Some extreme *look rich* people approach their retirement years with dread because without their income they have little else to live on. Their future may involve selling the cars and trading down to a smaller house in a less-fashionable suburb in order to raise money to cover living costs.

The High-Income *Look Rich* Person

A high-income person can still be a *look rich* person—the only difference between a low-income *look rich* person and a high-income *look rich* person is the scale of spending (notice in the diagrams the same amount going into the wealth box). To most observers, high-income *look rich* people seem fabulously wealthy because of their high-consumption lifestyles. In reality they may be only a pay packet or two away from poverty.

Fig. 4.3 HIGH-INCOME *LOOK RICH* MONEY FLOW

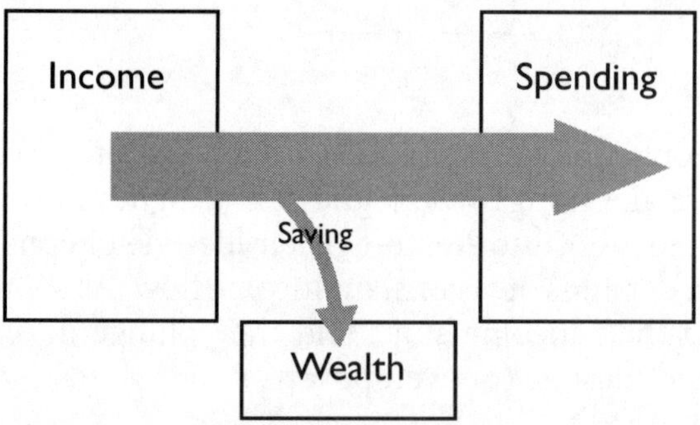

A recent newspaper article described a young woman who drives a BMW, plays golf on weekends and spends her holidays abroad. You might think that she is a wealthy professional, or a successful business owner. She is actually a young Japanese woman who is typical of ten million young Japanese consumers who live at home with their parents to avoid the high cost of housing. She has a temporary job and spends most of her income on personal consumption. Despite a sluggish Japanese economy, young

Japanese women are spending up big on fashionable clothes, trendy restaurants, travel, cars and club memberships. Their *look rich* lifestyle is making many shopkeepers smile but it is doing nothing for the women's long-term wealth.

The need to gain status and impress others are key features of the *look rich* lifestyle, yet they do not represent the last stage in Maslow's hierarchy of needs. Maslow would say that the *look rich* lifestyle cannot satisfy human needs in itself. He maintains that even when we have status and acceptance we are driven on by new needs, including the need to develop as a person. He calls this 'self-actualisation'. Of course, you can develop as a person while driving a Ferrari and living in a mansion, but it can be rather difficult if you are consumed by the need to earn in order to support your flash lifestyle.

For You To Do...

1. **What are the similarities between a low-income *look rich* person and a high-income *look rich* person?**
2. **What are the differences between them?**
3. **Make a list of the types of items high-income *look rich* people would spend their money on.**

The *Be Rich* Option

What is the alternative? Instead of trying to look rich, some Australians devote their energy to *becoming* rich—these are the *be rich* people. You may not notice a *be rich* person because he or she is not driven by the need to impress you with success. The *be rich* person might live in a comfortable but ordinary house, drive a regular family sedan and wear clothes that aren't the latest fashion. *Be rich* people are not motivated by a need to gain your admiration and approval. They may be motivated by a need to create a business from scratch, or to achieve a goal, or to become financially independent.

Figure 4.4 *LOOK RICH VERSUS BE RICH*

Not all people who aim to be rich will make it into the category of 'millionaire'. In the USA, the richest country in the world, only 3.50% of households have a net worth of over one million dollars. In early 2000 there were 4,000,000 millionaires and 170 billionaires in the USA. Australia has much more modest numbers; 240,000 millionaires, which is 1.26% of the entire population. While many of us won't make it into this exclusive club, we can, with a bit of effort, accumulate much more wealth than most other Australians with the same income as ourselves.

Millionaires are worth considering because they are the very successful end of the group who set out to be rich rather than look rich. After 20 years interviewing and surveying millionaires in the USA, two American academics have published their results in a book. The book—entitled *The Millionaire Next Door* (Stanley and Danko, 1998)—is worth reading by anyone who is interested in serious wealth.

Most American millionaires are first-generation rich. There will always be some millionaires who got started with a million or two from their parents, but believe it or not, over 80% of millionaires in the United States have started with nothing and built their wealth over a lifetime. Most people have heard of the fabulously wealthy Microsoft chief, Bill Gates, however American millionaires are not the technological whiz kids you might imagine. In fact many of their businesses are decidedly unromantic—they are in businesses such as truck part recycling, kitchen and bathroom supplies, equipment rental, real estate management or pest control.

No similar study has been done in Australia but the two societies are comparable, and individual cases in Australia bear out the general American pattern.

A subsequent survey by Stanley found that among the 733 millionaire respondents:

- 32% were business owners or entrepreneurs
- 16% were senior corporate executives
- 10% were attorneys
- 9% were physicians
- 33% were retirees, corporate middle managers, accountants, sales professionals, engineers, architects, teachers, professors or housewives.

While it is obvious that millionaires generally come from occupational groups that generate a high level of income, this alone will not make you rich. There is no single business or profession that will make you rich—but there is an attitude that will.

The *Be Rich* Money Flow

Just as the *look rich* people had their own money flow pattern (regardless of their occupation or level of income), so to do the *be rich* people. The money flow of the *be rich*, including the millionaires, is shown on the following page.

Figure 4.5 *BE RICH* MONEY FLOW

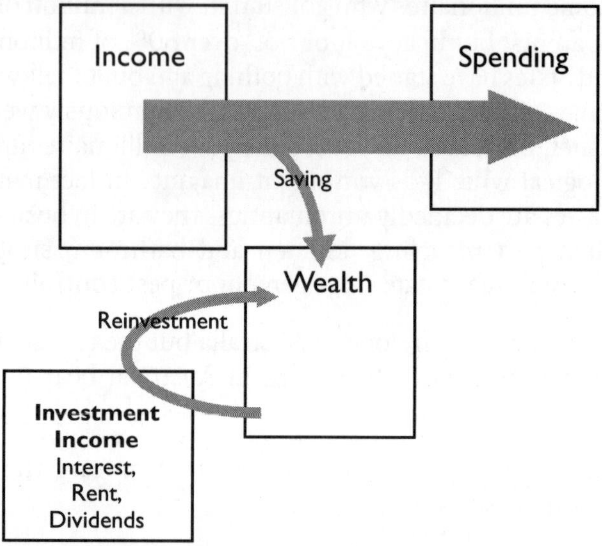

The *be rich* have a money flow that differs from the *look rich* in one important way; some of their income is diverted as savings into the wealth pool in a way that produces more income, which can then be reinvested. As the wealth pool grows it produces income such as interest on money lent to others, rents from property, and dividends or capital growth from shares. This income is then reinvested to make the wealth pool grow even faster. They have set up a continuous cycle of saving and reinvestment which will produce a large wealth pool over time.

For You To Do...

1. What are the essential differences between the money flows of the *look rich* and the *be rich*?
2. From what you have read so far, make up some rules for becoming rich. (Hint: think about income/ expenses; about saving; about what to do with income from investments.)

How Much is 'Wealthy'?

Remember that not all *be rich* people end up becoming millionaires, but they do end up a lot wealthier than other people on the same income level. How wealthy they become is influenced by how big their income is, and how long they have been receiving that income. It would be unreasonable to expect a young worker to have as much wealth as an older worker who has been earning for years. Similarly it would not be reasonable to expect a low-paid process worker to have as much wealth as a well-paid professional.

Stanley and Danko suggest a formula that provides a guide to a person's expected level of wealth accumulation:

(Age × Pre-tax household income) ÷ 10

Using this formula, people who have been in the workforce for some time can calculate the average or expected level of wealth accumulation for their age and income level.

For You To Do...

Calculate the expected wealth accumulation for the following people:

1. Mary and John are 35-year-old unskilled workers and their combined household income is $50,000.
2. Roger is a self-employed professional whose wife is not earning an income while she raises their children. Roger is 35 years old and has an annual income of $85,000.
3. Carlos is 29 and single. His annual income is $42,000.
4. Susan is a 23-year-old receptionist who earns $28,000 per annum.

Many *look rich* people have *less than half* the expected level of wealth for their age and income bracket. To be in the top 25% of wealth accumulators for your age and income (a *be rich* person) you need to have *twice* the figure calculated for your age and income.

Most first-generation millionaires are in the upper bracket, with more than twice the expected wealth accumulation for a person of their age and income. The upper bracket is also where you will find comparatively wealthy members of any income group. Being wealthy or being rich does not have to mean reaching a pre-set dollar target, it means *being wealthy in relation to your age and income level.* This should be achievable by everybody.

Figure 4.6 THE *BE RICH* AND THE *LOOK RICH*

Being Frugal

After countless interviews with self-made millionaires, Stanley and Danko concluded that "being frugal is the cornerstone of wealth building". 'Frugal' is an interesting word; it means sparing, thrifty, economical, careful. Basically what the *be rich* do is ensure that the money outflows (spending) are significantly smaller than the money inflows (income), i.e. they are frugal. The difference between their income and spending is then diverted into a growing pool of wealth.

The survey of the millionaires showed that the *be rich* people diverted at least 15% of their total income into wealth creation and lived on 85% of their total income. Most of them were careful budgeters, watching where the household dollars went each week. Those who did not budget made sure that they diverted at least 15% of their income into investments *before* they began spending their money. That way, when the money ran out—as it always does—their investment program was safe and they simply had to wait or save up for that item they couldn't yet afford.

Figure 4.7 HOW THE *BE RICH* ACCUMULATE WEALTH

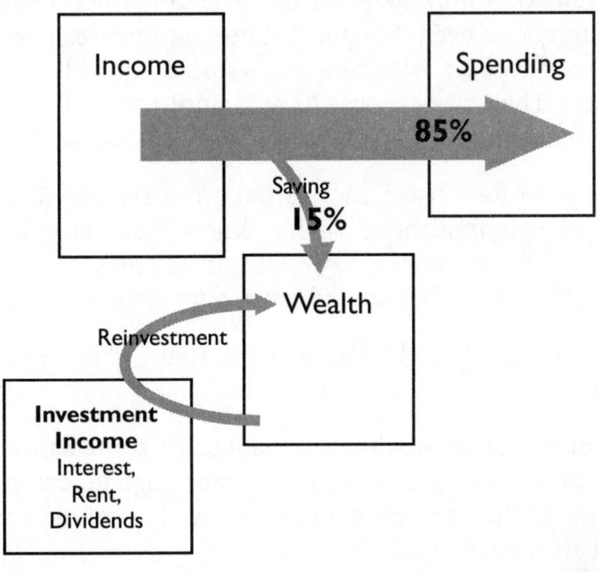

Living a careful and frugal lifestyle does not seem to bother the *be rich* people because their main motivation is to achieve, to create wealth, to build something from scratch or to become financially independent. On the other hand the *look rich* people are mainly motivated by a need to display a high-status lifestyle and impress other people. The *look rich* people find it almost impossible to create a wealth pool because most of what they earn each year is spent in supporting their expensive lifestyle, with its impressive house, cars, clothes and holidays.

Regularly saving 15% of your income might seem a difficult task, but the self-made millionaires often had simple and sensible ways of doing it. Remember that these examples come from *millionaire* business men and women. What makes them different to their peers in similar businesses or occupations is their ability to keep 15% or more of what they earn. They rarely had their clothes made by tailors, whereas their *look rich* business friends often did. Instead of exclusive or high-fashion clothes, they shopped for quality and durability. They drove a near-new ordinary model sedan, not an imported luxury car. The *look rich*, who need to demonstrate how successful they are, often spent a large amount of their income on new, imported luxury cars. (It is significant that two-thirds of those who drive luxury imported cars in the USA are *not* millionaires.) Some millionaires even thought that buying a new car was a waste of resources because new cars lost value so quickly in the first three years. Their strategy was to wait until a model was three or four years old and pick it up cheaply while it still had low kilometres.

Millionaires often lived in ordinary houses in older, well-established neighbourhoods—they knew that living in a posh neighbourhood or a new luxury estate created pressures for luxury cars, fashionable clothes and expensive recreation.

This economical lifestyle was so clear that Stanley and Danko developed a rule:

> **"If you're not yet wealthy but want to be some day, never purchase a house that requires a mortgage (a loan from the bank) that is more than twice your household's total annual income."**

In the Australian context house prices in some capital cities would make it difficult for the average wage earner to stick to this rule. The underlying principle is clear however—don't divert too much of your income into lifestyle goods at the expense of investments.

For You To Do...

Imagine you wanted to become one of the *be rich* people:

1. Make a list of the advantages of *not* living in a high-status neighbourhood.
2. If you run a business, what would be an advantage of *not* arriving at work in a very expensive luxury car?
3. What would be an advantage of *not* being drawn into a fashion competition with your friends?

Making Wealth Grow

So far you might have gained the impression that the *be rich* simply save a large pile of money and sit around counting it. Nothing could be further from the truth. Remember that you can rent your money to someone who needs it, just as easily as you can rent a spare house you might own. That's what the *be rich* do; they make sure their wealth works hard for them and grows in the process.

How they make their wealth grow will be discussed in more detail in Chapter 7. At present all you need to understand is that the *be rich* make their money work hard for them. In return they receive interest, rent or dividends (a share of the profits of companies they invest in). These provide another source of income.

However, as their aim is to grow their wealth, they do not spend this extra income (yet), they pour it back into the pool. This is called reinvesting the income. Every year that this cycle continues the pool grows larger.

Why Grow the Wealth Pool?

Now you know that the *be rich* make their wealth pool grow, but you don't really know their reasons for doing so. Do they do it just to feel rich? Do they do it for the pleasure of looking at a fat bank balance? Perhaps some do.

One reason why you might go to all this trouble to save and grow a wealth pool can be found in the investment income flow. Look at the *be rich* money flow below.

People with this flow have accumulated a wealth pool that produces an investment income which is equal to their regular salary or income. At this point they can quit their regular job and allow their wealth pool to support them for the rest of their lives! If you have ever heard of someone 'retiring early' chances are that their money flow looks like Figure 4.8.

Figure 4.8
THE MONEY FLOW FROM A LARGE WEALTH POOL

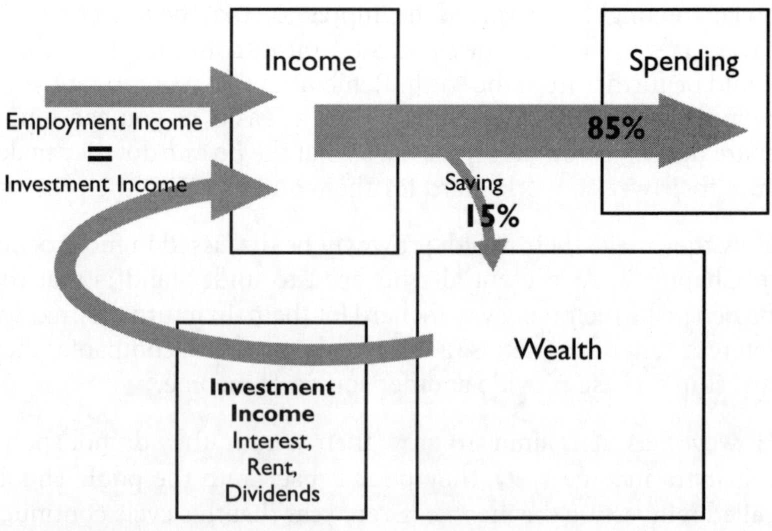

Having a wealth pool income equal to your regular salary (or at least big enough to live on) is what is meant by 'financial independence'. In practical terms it means freedom to do what you like—to work or not to work, to quit and pursue your hobbies or to continue doing what you do because you love it, not because you have to.

So now we know some of the reasons to be rich rather than just look rich. Think back to the interviews with people who won lotto (Chapter 1). When asked what they would do with all their money they replied that they would pay off the mortgage, take a trip, quit work, and help other people. You can spend your life hoping that you will have a huge lotto win, or you can start to grow a wealth pool—the choice is yours.

As one millionaire who grew up on a farm said:

> "My family understood the value of a dollar. Dad used to say seeds are a lot like dollars. You can eat the seeds or sow them. But when you see what seeds turn into—ten foot high corn—you don't want to waste them. Consume them or plant them. I always get a kick out of watching things grow" (Stanley and Danko, 1998).

Chapter Summary

- The *look rich* spend most or all of what they earn; they want to display a high-status lifestyle.
- The *be rich* save at least 15% of their income and live frugally on the remaining 85%.
- The *be rich* don't burden themselves with unnecessary debt to get a house—they keep house debt to less than two years income.
- The *be rich* reinvest the income from their investments to make their wealth pool grow faster.
- The *be rich* reach the stage where their wealth pool generates enough income to replace their regular salary.

Chapter 5

Starting the Wealth Pool

Think for a moment about a few of the key ideas touched on so far. A lot of money flows through our fingers in a lifetime. We can place this money under three headings:

- The money we get (our *income*).
- The money that goes out (our *spending*).
- The money we keep (our *savings*).

Keeping some of your money is not easy. In fact the majority of Australians keep very little of their income. One study of Australians' saving habits reported that if you took 100 people aged 20, and visited them 45 years later when they have just reached retirement age, you would find:

- 28 will be dead.
- 54 will be broke or on a pension—meaning they will be poor because the pension is only worth a quarter of the average weekly wage.
- 9 will still be working and living on low to average incomes.
- 8 will be living on a comfortable income.
- 1 will be rich.

This paints a pretty gloomy picture of our ability to save. We Australians are not alone in this inability to build wealth. The median (middle of the range) American household has a wealth of only $15,000 when you take out their home ownership. If you take out cars and furniture the average American is practically penniless (Stanley & Danko, 1998).

Why Aren't We Better at Saving?

One reason that we are not better at saving is that we confuse our 'needs' and our 'wants'. A 'need' is something we *must* have. There are only a small number of real needs in our lives. We need oxygen or we will die; we need food or we will die; we need fresh water or we will die; in most climates we need shelter and clothing or we will die. Beyond that it is hard to think of any real survival needs. When there is a flood or an earthquake people lose their telephones, houses, televisions, CD players, books, computers, cars, bicycles, furniture and dozens of other items. The emergency aid flows in from other communities and what we see coming off the Red Cross helicopters are tents, blankets, food and fresh water. These are what people *need*.

What we 'want' is another matter entirely. Our 'wants' are limitless. If you think of electronic entertainment gadgets alone, since your grandparents' time the average household has gone from wanting a radio to wanting:

- A black and white television
- A portable (transistor) radio
- A record player
- A stereo record player
- A colour television
- A video recorder
- A walkman radio

- A cassette player
- A walkman cassette player
- A CD player
- A portable CD player
- A computer
- A DVD player
- A digital camera
- A Sony Playstation.

There is no sign that this ever-growing series of wants is going to end. We will always want more because we are curious little animals who are fascinated with new toys. But once we have explored the latest wonder, we grow bored and seek the excitement of the next invention. This process of curiosity, wanting, then boredom is sped up by a very well paid and very clever group of people called advertisers. Their job is to convince you that what you *want* is actually something you *need*, and you should pay out your hard-earned cash to get it.

They do this in a host of clever ways. You have probably heard these arguments for spending your money on their product:

- Buy A and you will have fun.
- Buy B and you will be popular.
- Buy C and you will look attractive to the opposite sex.
- Buy D and you will be admired.
- Buy E and you will look successful.
- Buy F and you will feel good.

There is no doubt that powerful social pressures are against you when it comes to saving. To reduce your spending and increase your wealth you actually have to swim against the current of popular opinion and pressure.

For You To Do...

Write down your five most recent purchases, and then write down whether you consider each purchase to be a need or a want.

Put an approximate price on each want and estimate how many times you spend on this want in a year.

What is your total spending per year on these wants?

Strategies for Saving

Some people will read this and say to themselves, "Yes, I really should save more of my income...". Then immediately afterwards comes the "*...but...*". *But* I have these bills to pay; *but* I have to buy new clothes first; *but* I don't want to lead a miserable life of self-denial.

Then they hit on what seems to be a brilliant solution: "I can increase my savings and still keep my present level of spending if I can manage to increase my income." So they work harder, or look for a better paying job, or look for training which might bring promotion.

The problem with the 'work harder' solution is that it very rarely works! After working harder to gain more income we naturally feel that we deserve a reward, so we buy ourselves a little something. There is almost a law that says spending will always rise to match income; *more income = more spending*. Therefore; *more income ≠ more saving*.

The Solution: Pay Yourself First

Even those with the best of intentions often find that their income disappears and they have very little left over to put into savings. What they have been doing is using their income to pay for everything else first—food, transport, housing, entertainment—and hoping there will be something left over at the end to pay themselves.

You can get around this by arranging to pay yourself first; you can then spend whatever you have left. You can do this by having your employer put a set amount from your pay into an investment account, or you can arrange for your bank or building society to regularly pay a set amount into another account for investment purposes. If you are a student receiving money from your parents, you can arrange for them to bank a set percentage for you and give you the rest to spend.

The 'pay-yourself-first' strategy is used by people who do not want to keep track of every dollar in a family budget. The pay-yourself-first strategy forces you to limit your spending, simply because you run out of money. You may have to put off buying the new set of clothes until you have more cash. You may have to cook your own dinner instead of going out for a meal. You may have to plan ahead so that you can afford the tickets for a concert, and you may have to holiday closer to home instead of going to exotic locations.

Once it is in place, the arrangement to pay yourself first operates automatically, and most people who use it report that they quickly adjust to being a little more careful with their remaining income.

Can You Save Your Way to Wealth?

If you take this question literally the answer has to be "No, you can't save enough to become wealthy." For example, if you saved \$20 a week for 40 years you would have: $\$20 \times 52 \times 40 = \$41,600$. This amount of money is not to be sneezed at, but it will not make you rich after 40 years. Even if you triple the saving to \$60 per week you only end up with \$124,800.

At $20 a week you would have a fairly miserable $41,600 after 40 years of savings effort *if you kept the money in a bottom drawer or under the mattress.* But do you remember what you learned in Chapter 2? Your money is like a house; you can lend it to someone and charge interest (rent) on it. In this way, while you get on with your life, your money will be working for you to earn more money. Your wealth will be growing from two sources; the savings you are continually adding and the interest you are charging others for the use of your money.

Compound Interest

If you are aged 18 and you saved and invested $100 a month (or about $25 per week) at 11% per year you would have $1,083,077 to retire with at the age of 60. If you delayed *for just five years* and spent the money instead, you would have only $621,807 accumulated by the age of 60. The price you would pay for spending $25 per week for five years instead of investing it would be $461,270. These huge differences later in life that result from small differences early in life are the result of a magical thing called 'compound interest'.

If you place your money in a bank account it will earn interest each year. If you reinvest this interest you start the next year with a larger pool, which earns more interest than the previous year. If you reinvest the interest again at the end of the next year you create an even bigger pool, which earns even more interest...and on it goes. This process of reinvesting and earning interest on interest is known as compound interest. Figure 5.1 (opposite) shows what happens if you save $20 per week for a year, then stop saving and simply allow compound interest to do its work at 10% per year for five years.

Compound interest is often described as 'magical' because of the way it grows slowly at first and then grows at ever-increasing rates. Albert Einstein is supposed to have said that compound interest is the eighth wonder of the world.

Figure 5.1 10% COMPOUND INTEREST ON $1,040

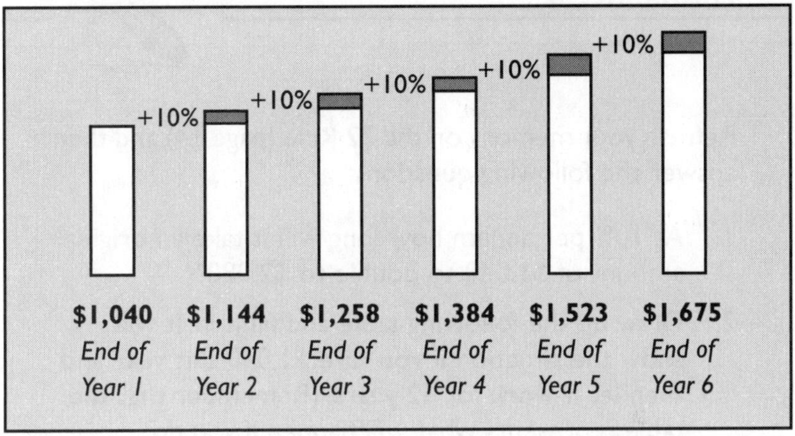

Compound interest is the biggest aid to wealth growth any young person can have. Most people don't understand compound interest until they look back from the age of 50 and see how much they have missed out. Understanding compound interest at 20 is far better than waiting until you are 50 and it's too late.

You can do compound interest calculations in your head by using the 72 Rule. At 10% interest an investment doubles every seven years, at 7% it doubles every ten years. The time an investment takes to double at various interest rates is shown below.

Table 5.1 INVESTMENT DOUBLING TIME

Interest Rate	*72 Rule*	*Time to double in value (years)*
6%	72 ÷ 6	12
7%	72 ÷ 7	10
8%	72 ÷ 8	9
9%	72 ÷ 9	8
10%	72 ÷ 10	7

For You To Do...

Refresh your memory on the 72 Rule (page 14) and then answer the following questions:

1. At 10% per annum how long will it take an original amount of $1,040 to double to $2,080?

2. Draw up the following table and fill it in. It will show the situation if you save $1,040 this year and then let it work for 42 years. (Remember that the table represents what will happen if you do nothing apart from save the original $1,040.)

Years After Beginning	*Value of Investment Compounding at 10% p.a. ($)*
1 Year	
7 Years	
14 Years	
21 Years	
28 Years	
35 Years	
42 Years	

3. Plot the points from the table on a graph, with years along the horizontal axis and dollars along the vertical axis.

Join the points in a smooth curve. The graph should look similar to Figure 5.2.

4. From the table and the graph, what do you notice about the speed of growth in wealth?
5. Compare the total *increase* for the period 35 years to 42 years with the *total wealth accumulated* by 35 years. What do you notice?

If you have worked your way through the previous example you will understand a lot about compound interest. The first years show little wealth growth. This means that you have to be patient with compound interest. The rise in wealth is slow at first but becomes faster and faster. The people who really benefit from compound interest are the young, because they have the time for it to work its magic.

Even though interest rates go up and down, the shape of the compound interest graph always follows the same pattern—slow at first then rising more and more steeply. This is shown below.

Figure 5.2 COMPOUND INTEREST GRAPH

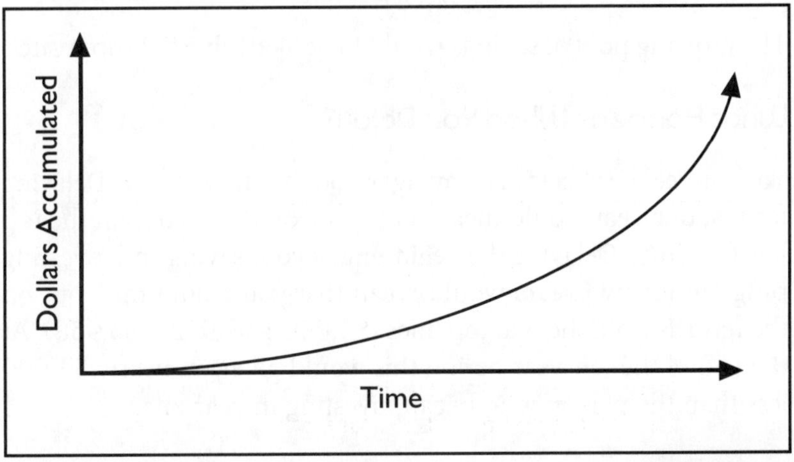

Compound Interest Plus Regular Saving

So far the examples of compound interest have been of the 'set and forget' variety—money was invested and allowed to grow by reinvesting the interest each year. Most investors don't make a 'one-off' investment, however, unless it is an inheritance from a rich relative or some other one-off occurrence. Instead, they save regularly (or irregularly) into their investment pool. The result is a wealth pool that is growing because new savings are being added, and compound interest is therefore having an effect on an ever-increasing amount of money.

You can understand the combined impact of savings and compound interest if you imagine a simplified case where an investor, Rebecca, invests her savings at the end of every year in a new account. Assume that she can only save $20 per week. This adds up to $1,040 in a year. How much would she have at the end of ten years after banking just this amount? If the $1,040 was invested for ten years (at 7% per annum) Rebecca would end up with $2,046. However, she is also saving during the second year and invests another $1,040 at the end of that year. This also grows at a compound interest rate and will increase to $1,912 by the tenth year. She saves a further $1,040 during the third year and invests it...and so on for ten years, saving and investing each year.

The growing pool of savings would look like Table 5.2 (opposite).

What Happens When You Delay?

You can see the effects of delaying by looking at Table 5.2. Delaying for just one year would mean that you would miss out on the top line ($2,046). Delaying the beginning of your saving and investing program for two years would mean that you would miss out on the returns from the two top lines ($2,046 + $1,912 = $3,958). At the end of the ten-year period this would give you nearly $4,000 less than the person who began investing in year one.

Table 5.2 SAVINGS AND COMPOUND INTEREST

Year	Amount Invested	Amount After Ten Years
1	$1,040	$2,046
2	$1,040	$1,912
3	$1,040	$1,787
4	$1,040	$1,671
5	$1,040	$1,494
6	$1,040	$1,363
7	$1,040	$1,274
8	$1,040	$1,191
9	$1,040	$1,113
10	$1,040	$1,040
Total:	$10,400	$14,891

In Table 5.2, each year $1,040 is saved (which is $20 per week) and invested until year ten. The year ten total ($14,891) will be the sum of all the yearly savings plus the compound interest on each amount. Rebecca has contributed a total of $10,400 ($1,040 × 10), while interest has contributed $4,491 ($14,891 – $10,400). This is a 43% return on her savings.

Time is the key for compound interest. People who put off saving while they spend on a flash lifestyle are *look rich* people. By the time they wake up—if they ever do—precious years, or even decades, have been lost.

Imagine two *be rich* people, Adam and Andrea, on an ordinary income. They decided to begin saving as soon as they got their first part-time jobs at the age of 15. Their wealth pool would have 50 years to grow before they retired at 65.

Their friends—the *average* people—Brian and Betty were keen to enjoy the feeling of wealth their first jobs gave them and found many ways to spend all they earned. By the time they were 30 they decided to think seriously about the future and began saving. They were 15 years behind Adam and Andrea but it was still a long way to retirement—35 years.

Their other friends—the *look rich* people—Charles and Clarissa thought that there was plenty of time to settle down and save later. They spent most of their income and seemed to exist from pay packet to pay packet. They enjoyed living a high-status lifestyle and most of their friends thought that they were rich. About their forty-fifth birthdays, Charles and Clarissa thought they should be putting something away for their old age, and they began to save.

The six friends all had similar jobs and incomes. When they started saving, they all saved the same amount of money per week into a similar investment—they saved $50 per week and invested at 8% per annum. (As you will see in later chapters on investment, 8% is a quite conservative figure.) A graph of their savings would look like Figure 5.3.

Figure 5.3 BEGINNING AT DIFFERENT TIMES

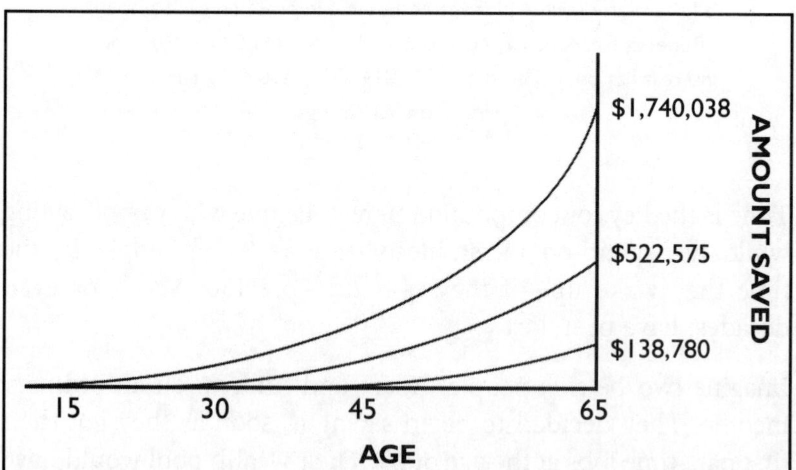

Notice that all three graph lines follow the same path. They are not parallel because progress is slower at the beginning and speeds up later. Despite the difference in the look of the lines, all the savings are growing at the same percentage rate. The difference is time! Having lost so much time, Charles and Clarissa will find it almost impossible to catch up with Adam and Andrea.

The different financial fates of the three couples is even more dramatic if you look at the cost of delaying and the return on their savings, shown in Table 5.3.

Table 5.3 RETURNS ON SAVINGS

	Adam & Andrea	Bill & Betty	Charles & Clarissa
Started Saving at	15	30	45
Amount at Age 65	$1,740,038	$522,575	$138,780
Cost of Delaying	–	$1,217,463	$1,601,258
Total Savings Input	$130,000	$91,000	$52,000
Return for Every $1.00 Saved	$13.38	$5.74	$2.67

Table 5.3 calculated on saving $50 per week until age 65 and investing at 8% per annum compound. Tax and inflation have not been included.

For Bill and Betty the cost of delaying just 15 years, until they were 30 years old, is a whopping $1,217,463. This may seem incredible but it is not so strange if you think of the 72 Rule.

With a return of 8% per annum, Adam and Andrea's wealth will double about every nine years (72 ÷ 8 = 9), so in the 15 years Bill and Betty delayed Adam and Andrea's wealth had undergone 1.66 doublings (15 ÷ 9). This makes a huge difference, especially at the end when the pool of money to be doubled is already high.

The longer compound interest has to work the more it will contribute to the total at the end. Adam and Andrea saved the most ($130,000) over their working lives and they accumulated over one-and-a-half million dollars ($1,740,038)—that's a return of $13.38 for every $1.00 saved. Charles and Clarissa saved the least ($52,000) and they only received $2.67 back for every $1.00 saved.

The Rate of Return

You have just read about the vast differences in the retirement wealth of three couples simply because of the different lengths of time they had been saving and investing. There is a second, almost as powerful, factor which will influence their final level of wealth; the rate of return they get on their investments. In later chapters you will learn more about the different rates of return to be expected from investment options, as well as how to magnify that return by using borrowed money. For now, let's just imagine that our fictitious couples all saved the same amounts as before, but gained higher rates of return on their investments each year. The previous example was calculated on an 8% annual return. What would their retirement wealth be if they received 10% or 12% returns?

For Adam and Andrea, who saved and invested the longest, improving their rate of return by a mere 50% (from 8% up to 12%) more than quadruples their final payout—a huge 450% increase.

Table 5.4 THE EFFECTS OF INTEREST RATES

	Adam & Andrea	Bill & Betty	Charles & Clarissa
Started Saving at	15	30	45
Amount at Age 65 @ 8% p.a.	$1,740,038	$522,575	$138,780
Amount at Age 65 @ 10% p.a.	$3,661,656	$852,643	$180,187
Amount at Age 65 @ 12% p.a.	$7,827,515	$1,407,844	$234,994
Total Savings Input	$130,000	$91,000	$52,000

Tax and inflation have not been included.

You can compare a 'best case' with a 'worst case' to see the dramatic effects of time and interest rates. Assume Charles and Clarissa started late and earned a low rate of return (8%); they would have accumulated a mere $138,780 to retire on. Assume Adam and Andrea started early and sought a high rate of return (12%). As a result, they retired with nearly $8,000,000, or around 56 times the wealth of Charles and Clarissa! The *look rich* life choice comes with a very big price tag!

You can draw a basic saving and investment rule from these couples:

> The people who end up with the most wealth will be those who save and invest for the longest time, at the highest rate.

Calculating Compound Interest

You can calculate the amount of compound interest you will earn on any amount of money with the help of a scientific calculator. The formula is:

$$A = P\,(1 + \frac{r}{100})^n$$

In the formula, *A* is the value of the original amount *P* after *n* periods at *r* rate of interest.

For example, what would an original investment of $2,000 be worth in 25 years if the interest rate was 8%?

$$A = 2{,}000 \times (1 + 0.08)^{25}$$

$$A = 2{,}000 \times (1.08)^{25}$$

To calculate $(1.08)^{25}$ enter [1][.][0][8], press the [Y^x] key, and then enter [2][5]. This will give you 6.8484.

$$(1.08)^{25} = 6.8484$$

$$A = 2{,}000 \times 6.8484$$

$$A = \$13{,}696.95$$

In 25 years time the $2,000 will have grown to $13,697 simply by reinvesting the interest.

Chapter Summary

- Distinguish between a want and a need if you aim to become wealthy.
- Pay yourself first—arrange for a set percentage of your income to be invested before you get your hands on it and spend.
- Compound interest is magic if it is given time—so start early.
- Compound interest and regular savings contribute significantly to your wealth growth.
- The rate of return on investments has a significant impact on the final outcome from a lifetime of saving and investing—so aim for high rates.

Chapter 6

Debt

Most of us have been in debt at some stage in our lives. We usually get into debt when we want something but we don't have the money to pay for it. Rather than wait for our next payment—whether it be pocket money or wages or income from other sources—we go to someone who has spare money and ask to borrow some. So a child might go to his or her mother and say, "Mum, I need to buy new t-shirt. Can you lend me some of my pocket money now and I'll pay you back on Saturday?" Mothers are usually softhearted, and as long as the money is for something reasonable they will give the child a loan which can be paid back later (and they probably won't charge interest!).

For some people this simple childhood transaction sets the pattern for their life with money: if I don't have enough money to buy it now, I will go to people with spare money and use their money instead. But there is one little difference in the adult world—they are likely to charge you for the use of their money! You are actually renting their money for a while and you will be expected to give it back with a fee for its use. The fee is called interest. So, in the adult world, borrowing money costs you. When you buy something with borrowed money you pay for both the item and for the use of the borrowed money. Furthermore, because charging interest is profitable there will be people lining up to lend you money. You can borrow money from credit card companies, finance companies, credit unions and banks. They don't do it because you have a nice smile, they lend money in order to make money from you!

Past generations had no doubt about the fact that debt was to be avoided at all costs. In Shakespeare's play *Hamlet* the old man Polonius advises his son to "neither a borrower nor a lender be". You will still find many people, particularly in the older generations, who have a deep dislike for debt. If only it was that simple, we could end this chapter here by saying "Don't do it!".

Life is more complex than that, though. In this chapter you will learn that there is 'good' debt, 'not-so-good' debt and 'bad' debt. I have put these descriptions in inverted commas because they sound like moral judgements and they are not really. Debt is only good or bad insofar as it helps you reach your goals. Some debt can be a great help while other debt can weigh you down and stop you from reaching your goals. To know which is which you need to see debt in the big picture (i.e. how it relates to your money flow), and you will also need to know the differences between types of debt.

Debt and Your Money Flow

To really understand the impact of borrowing you need to have a clear idea of where debt fits into the big picture of your finances. Figure 6.1 shows how debt affects your money flow.

Paying for debt can soak up the spare money you might otherwise be directing into your wealth pool. Because it stops you saving, debt can delay the growth of your wealth pool. If you think of the examples from the previous chapter of compound interest at work, you can see that any delay has a big price tag in the long run.

Fig. 6.1 DEBT CAN DELAY YOUR WEALTH CREATION

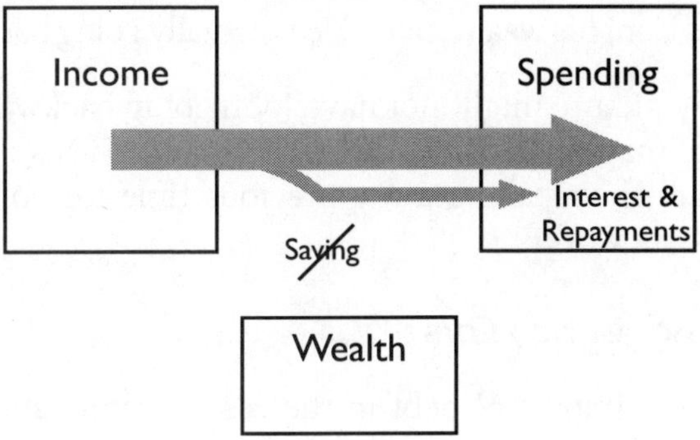

For some people, debt can have an even more devastating impact. It can actually reverse the money flow to the wealth pool and make them draw on their savings to service the debt. Figure 6.2 illustrates the money flow of John, who has become badly indebted and has to draw on his wealth to service the loan. In this situation, debt is actually making John poorer as time goes on.

Figure 6.2 DEBT CAN MAKE YOU POOR

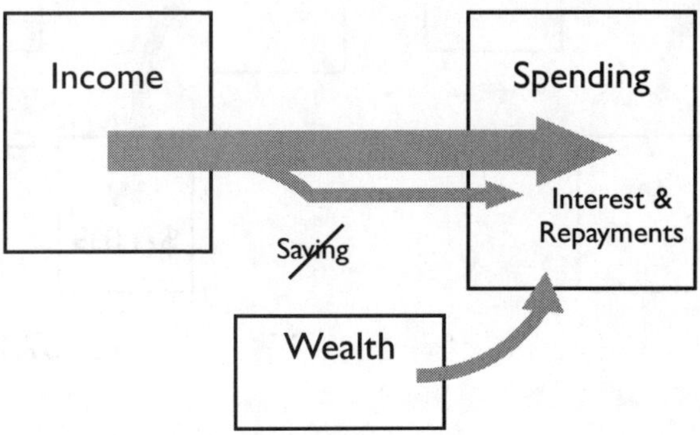

For John the money needed to pay back the borrowed money plus interest has used so much of his income that he has to top-up the payments from his wealth pool. He is actually going backwards.

A less gloomy picture might not have John going backwards into poverty. Debt may simply slow down the amount he can channel into the wealth box, taking away precious time for compound interest to do its work.

Jenny and Roger Buy Cars

You can see the impact of debt in the case of Jenny and Roger. They both began working after leaving school at the age of 18. Jenny saved and bought a small second-hand car for $3,000. Roger also saved $3,000 but he bought a new car for $25,000, with a $22,000 loan from a finance company at 10% interest. Roger choose the ten-year repayment plan to keep the repayments at a low $67.09 per week. When they were both 28 years old Roger had paid out a total of $34,887.60 and he owned a ten-year-old car.

Figure 6.3 MONEY FLOWS FOR ROGER AND JENNY

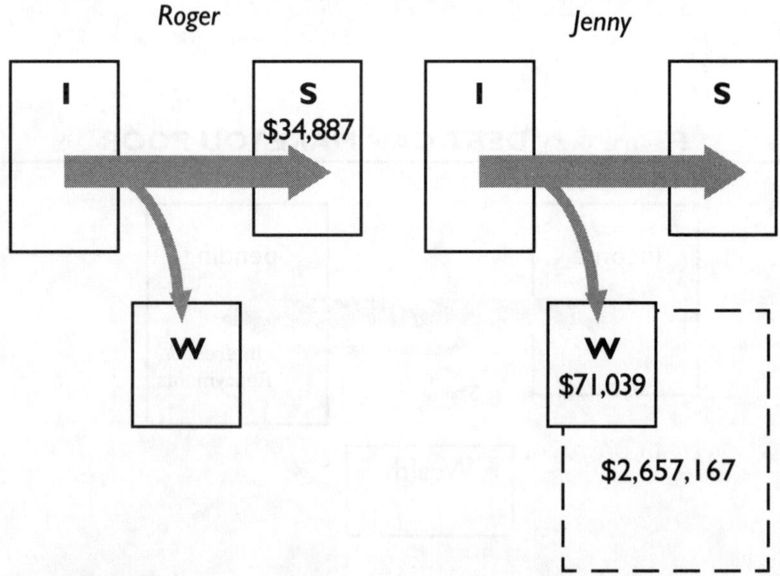

During the ten years Roger had been paying off his car at around $67 per week, Jenny had been investing $67 per week at 10% per annum. She now had a very old car and more than $71,039 in investments!

If Jenny stopped saving at the age of 28 and simply allowed her wealth pool to grow at 10% per annum for the rest of her working life, how much would she have to retire on at the age of 65? Remember, this is *without any saving* after the age of 28.

The answer is $2,657,167 (this amount assumes that no tax is paid on dividends).

The real cost of Roger's debt was the lost opportunity to save into his wealth pool and allow compound interest to do its work. By the age of 28 Roger had driven a new—but steadily aging—car for ten years. It cost him the opportunity to save $71,039—and it also cost him $2,657,167 to retire on. That was a very expensive car! No doubt young Roger would have looked at you in disbelief if you had tried to convince him that his new car would eventually cost him over two-and-a-half million dollars.

Understanding debt will help you avoid this situation. And to fully understand debt you need to be aware that there are actually three types of debt.

Three Types of Debt

The three types of debt are:

1. We can borrow money to buy something which will go down in value (called a depreciating asset).
2. We can borrow to buy something which will go up in value (an appreciating asset).
3. We can borrow to buy something which will go up in value (an appreciating asset) and ensure that there are tax benefits as well.

We will look at each of these individually.

Borrowing to Buy a Depreciating Asset

We can borrow to buy airline tickets for a holiday. Three weeks later they are worthless and we still have a debt to repay. We can borrow money to buy clothes, but as soon as we wear them they are second-hand and worth only half as much. Fairly soon they will be out of fashion and we still have a debt to repay. We can borrow for big items such as a car, but as soon as it is driven out of the showroom it drops in value and continues to drop in value every year—and we still have a debt to repay.

There may be times in life when you have no alternative but to borrow money to buy a depreciating asset. You might write-off your car in a crash, but your job depends on you being mobile and you haven't enough spare cash to buy a replacement, so you have to borrow. Your new car is going down in value while you are repaying the loan and interest to the bank. In the end you are left with a much less valuable car and an empty wallet.

Borrowing to Buy an Appreciating Asset

Most Australians want to own their own home. For many people this is the largest single purchase they will ever make and they make it at a time when they are just starting out on their adult lives. Of course very few can afford to pay cash for their house, town house, apartment or flat. They could save up over several years but inflation will be pushing up house prices as they try to gather the money to enter the market. So they turn to a bank, building society or mortgage lender and they borrow one hundred thousand dollars or more. This saddles them with a huge debt, but in some ways it is better than the first kind of debt because even though they have to pay a lot of interest for the use of the bank's money, their house is (almost always) growing in value. With a depreciating asset, such as a car, you end up with a less valuable item after you have paid out all the loan plus interest. With an appreciating asset such as a house, you end up with a more valuable item after repaying the loan plus interest. This makes it a better type of debt than one where you only have a worn out car or a few holiday shots to show for all your efforts!

Borrowing to Buy an Appreciating Asset with Tax Benefits

You know already that the government collects taxes from your income. However, if you had to spend money in order to gain that income you are able to claim the expense as a deduction and therefore pay less tax.

Sam is a tradesman who earns $30,000 a year. The tax department would calculate his tax on $30,000 and decide that he owes the government $5,379.53 in income tax. However, Sam has had to spend $4,000 on tools and equipment in order to earn his $30,000 income. To be fair to Sam the government rules that he can deduct these expenses from the total before the income tax is calculated. So now Sam is taxed on $26,000 ($30,000 – $4,000) because he deducted expenses that were necessary for him to earn his income. His new tax bill on $26,000 is $4,179.53.

Suppose Sam borrowed money to buy an investment that would make a rental income for him. The interest he paid on the borrowed money is an expense that he can deduct from his income before he works out how much tax he must pay. For instance, if Sam borrowed $100,000 to buy a shop, the bank will expect him to pay back the money with interest. Sam plans to rent the shop to a local business so that he gets a regular rental income from his investment. The rental income is taxed like any other income, but the interest charged by the bank can be claimed as a deduction. This means he can deduct the interest costs from his income before tax is calculated, meaning he pays less tax.

Debt on something that earns an income is different to debt on your own home: on your own home the tax department does not help you by reducing your tax. When paying off your own home you pay the full tax on your income and your repayments to the bank are made from your after-tax dollars.

So you can see that there are 'bad' debts where the value of the item purchased decreases while you are paying it off. There are 'not-so-good' debts where the value of the item increases as you pay it off and you end up with something worth more than it was in the beginning. Finally, there are 'good' debts where the tax department helps you pay off the debt and gain something of value which will provide you with an investment income (more about this type of debt in the following chapter).

The Cost of a Debt

Many people see debt as a simple way of getting what they want *now*. They never take the time to calculate the full cost of using someone else's money to fund their lifestyle. They look at the price of an item and think "I can afford that". It may not cross their minds that the real cost is:

Total cost = Cost of the item + Cost of the money

In fact, if you think of Roger and Jenny buying their cars, the total cost of Roger's car was:

The cost of the car + Cost of the money +
Lost opportunity to accumulate wealth

Another trap is to look only at the cost of each repayment. Advertisements for 'easy repayments' lure unsuspecting buyers to sign contracts which will commit them to a long and expensive process of repaying the loan and the interest. The loan repayments chart (on page 68) can help you see the real cost of an item. It shows the annual repayments on $1,000 at different interest rates and over different periods.

For You To Do...

1. **Imagine you want to buy a second-hand car. You don't have much money but the helpful dealer arranges finance from a finance company and you take out a $6,000 loan. The interest rate is 11.5% and you agree to pay over ten years.**

Using the loan repayments chart you can calculate the cost of your loan in the following way:

Step 1. Find the 11.5% interest rate in the left-hand column.

Step 2. Read across to the annual repayments on $1,000 for a ten-year loan.

Step 3. Multiply the figure from Step 2 by six to find the annual repayments for a $6,000 loan.

Step 4. Find the total payments by multiplying the annual repayments by ten for the ten years of payments.

Step 5. Take the loan amount ($6,000) away from the result of Step 4 to find how much you will pay in interest.

2. Instead of accepting the car dealer's kind offer of finance with the finance company you might shop around and discover that the local bank or credit union offered loans for cars at 10.5% (1.0% cheaper).

   Repeat steps 1 to 5 and find out how much you could save in interest payments with this loan.

3. Your parents are worried that you will be burdened with loan repayments for the next ten years and they advise you to get rid of the debt as quickly as possible. You have chosen the bank's loan at 10.5%. Repeat steps 1 to 5, but this time use the repayment amount for *five* years. (Remember you still multiply the amount on the chart by six because you borrowed $6,000.)

4. Summarise what you have learned about the amount of interest paid:

   - When you reduce the interest rate.
   - When you reduce the loan period.

Table 6.1 LOAN REPAYMENT CHART

	Term of Loan				
	5 Years	10 Years	15 Years	20 Years	25 Years
	Amount paid annually for each $1,000 borrowed				
Interest Rate	$	$	$	$	$
8.0%	243.31	145.59	114.67	100.37	92.61
8.25%	244.75	147.18	116.41	102.24	94.61
8.5%	246.19	148.78	118.16	104.13	96.62
8.75%	247.64	150.39	119.93	106.04	98.65
9.0%	249.10	152.01	121.71	107.96	100.70
9.25%	250.55	153.63	123.50	109.90	102.77
9.5%	252.02	155.27	125.31	111.86	104.84
9.75%	253.49	156.92	127.12	113.82	106.93
10.0%	254.96	158.58	128.95	115.80	109.04
10.5%	257.92	161.92	132.65	119.81	113.30
11.0%	260.90	165.30	136.39	123.86	117.61
11.5%	263.91	168.71	140.18	127.97	121.98
12.0%	266.93	172.16	144.02	132.13	126.39
12.5%	269.97	175.65	147.90	136.33	130.84
13.0%	273.03	179.17	151.82	140.58	135.34
13.5%	276.11	182.72	155.79	144.88	139.87
14.0%	279.21	186.31	159.80	149.22	144.45
14.5%	282.33	189.94	163.86	153.59	149.05
15.0%	285.47	193.60	167.45	158.01	153.69

Beware the Plastic Debt Trap

You know now that the worst kind of debt is debt on items that decrease in value (depreciating assets). Would it surprise you that many Australians have slipped into this kind of debt by borrowing for food, clothing, holidays, entertainment and dozens of other items? They did this through a small plastic card.

To understand 'plastic money' you need to know that there are two kinds of cards—debit cards and credit cards.

Debit Cards

A debit card allows you to use the money you already have in your account to pay for items by Electronic Funds Transfer at the Point Of Sale (EFTPOS). Many people use their debit card instead of carrying cash around with them. They can also use it to withdraw cash from their account by using an Automatic Teller Machine (ATM). The key point is that a debit card uses *your* money, not somebody else's. With a debit card the worst that can happen is that your account runs out of money and you suffer the embarrassment of not being able to pay at the shop.

Credit Cards

A credit card is a different kettle of fish altogether. With a credit card you borrow money from someone else—a bank, a credit union or a finance company. Depending on your age and income, the credit card provider will place a credit limit on your card. This means that you are only allowed to borrow up to that limit. In late 2000 Australians had accumulated sixteen billion dollars in credit card debt. That's *sixteen thousand million dollars*!

There are two main types of credit cards.

No Interest-Free Period Card

The first type charges you interest from the date you buy an item. They have no annual fee and they generally have a lower rate of interest. You have to pay off at least 5% of the total debt at the end of each month. Companies offering this type of card make their money by you staying 95% in debt from month to month. In January 1999 owners of all types of credit cards put four billion dollars worth of new debt on their cards. This was on top of six billion dollars carried over from previous months.

Cards With Interest-Free Periods

The second type of card offers an interest-free period, but charges you an annual fee (generally about $25) and has a higher rate of interest. If you are well-organised and very self-disciplined you can arrange to pay off your accumulated debt before the interest-free period is over. In that way you have had the use of the credit card's money for a month or more without paying any interest.

Cash Advances

Both types of cards allow you to obtain cash advances—you can borrow cash for whatever you want simply by presenting your card. But cash advances are treated differently to other purchases. Interest is charged from day one, from when you receive the cash advance—even if you have one of the cards with an interest-free period on other purchases. Many people don't know or don't care about the difference between the treatment of purchases and that of cash advances, and they pay the price. In one month (January 1999) Australians took out $430,000,000 in cash advances—75% of this was on cards with an interest-free period, the type of cards which charge higher interest rates. This 75% ($322,500,000) in credit was borrowed at a higher rate of interest until the card owners paid off *all* the debt owing on the card. The interest payments on carried-over debt in Australia were almost $90,000,000!

So you can spot the trap. It's just too easy, isn't it? You go shopping with your little plastic card in your pocket. You spot something nice and—no money?—no problems, you don't have to pay until the end of the month. It can get worse. At the end of the month you have the choice of paying off the whole debt or paying off 5% and rolling over the 95% into the following month. Guess what many people do?

The Debt Spiral

If you pay your 5% regularly you are a good, reliable customer, so you will have no trouble getting a second card from another company (or the same company). Spend up to the credit limit, pay your 5% each month, and you are still a good customer so you can get a third card. If you do this, however, your debt can quickly become a major financial problem. At this point you might seek advice and be told to convert all your little debts into one big debt, called a consolidation loan. This doesn't take away your debt problem, it just brings it all together (although it may reduce the number of fees you have to pay). It may take you years to repay the consolidation loan and by that time all the little items you bought on credit will be worthless. Bad credit card debt is the ultimate depreciating-asset debt because very few of the items purchased will have any lasting value.

It helps to understand the danger of credit card debt if you compare the cost of borrowing money from different sources, as shown in Table 6.2. You can see how high the interest rates are on the credit cards. (These figures are accurate for April, 2000. They may go up or down but the differences between the debt types stays fairly constant.)

Table 6.2 BORROWING FROM DIFFERENT SOURCES

	Interest rate (%)	Total repayments on $1,000 borrowed for one year at highest interest rate
Home loan; bank mortgage; standard variable rate	6.99 to 7.65	$1,076.50
Personal loan; bank standard variable rate	11.70	$1,117.00
No interest-free period credit card	10.95 to 15.40	$1,154.00
Credit card with interest-free period	13.85 to 16.95	$1,169.50

Chapter Summary

Now that you understand more about debt we can make some simple debt rules:

- Try very, very, very, very hard to avoid debt on an item that loses value.
- Pay off debt as quickly as possible, even on an item which increases in value.
- Learn how tax-advantaged debt can help you build your wealth pool.
- Total debt costs increase when the interest rate rises or the term lengthens.
- Remember that the real cost of debt is often in lost opportunity—a small debt early in your adult life can end up costing a lot more later on.

Part Two

Investing Your Wealth

Chapter 7

An Overview of Investing

If you have managed to follow the book so far you are well on the way to becoming financially literate. That is, you know a little about the language of money and how money works in your life. The previous chapters told you about some of the choices you can make about money, choices such as:

- *Look rich* (spend now) or *be rich* (save and invest to grow wealth).
- Start now and let compound interest work for you or delay and grow much less wealth.
- Go into debt on depreciating assets or go into debt only on appreciating assets.

These chapters on investment provide you with information about another set of choices you have—the choices on how to make your wealth pool grow and work for you. What you do with this information will depend on your approach to life. Do you believe that you control your destiny or do you believe that things just happen to you? You will use the investment information as a starting point to wealth only if you believe that you are (at least partly) responsible for what happens to you. If you are a fatalist and think that you can't influence your future, then you had better stop here.

Certainly there is the possibility that you will be run over by a bus in ten years time—so why not spend, spend, spend and have a great time while you can? There is no convincing answer to someone who has this attitude to life. You *may* be run over by a bus, but you *probably* won't be. Do you want to run your life on a *possibility* or a *probability*? It's your choice.

If you have already decided to be responsible for your life you might have chosen to become a *be rich* person, to save a part of your income and to avoid debt on depreciating assets. *Good for you!* These decisions will have led to the beginning of a wealth pool. The question now becomes: "How do I make my small wealth pool into a big wealth pool?" You notice that the focus is on growing your wealth pool, not simply on where to keep it safe. A waterproof box under the vegetable garden might be safe, but you know what inflation is going to do to the value of your cache.

There are literally hundreds of different ways of growing your wealth. They can be simplified into two groups:

1. **Debt investments:** You lend your money to someone else and expect them to return it with interest.
2. **Equity investments:** Equity in this situation means 'ownership'. With equity investments you use your money to buy something which will increase in value over time—this is referred to as *capital growth*. Equity investments also provide *income*. Equity investments are usually either:
    - Shares, or
    - Property.

We will look at each of these in turn in the following chapters. Remember, however, that the purpose of this book is to introduce you to the way money works in your life—it does not set out to advise you on how to invest your money.

Why Should I Invest?

When you are ready to stop working at the age of 65 (or earlier) you have 20 or more years of your life left. What will happen in the last years of your life when there is no wage or salary flowing in each week? One way to gain some income is to rely on the community to look after you by paying you a pension. If you choose this path you will be living on an income that is fixed at 25% of the average weekly wage—not much luxury there.

The alternative to a government pension is to rely on the income flow from your investments. If that money flow equals your regular employment income by the time you are 40 or 50 you have the choice of retiring early.

Except for the few who inherit wealth from their parents or are lucky enough to have a large gambling win, all wealth begins with employment generating an income. Once you begin generating an income the vital *look rich* or *be rich* choice arises.

As we saw in Chapter 2, the *look rich* choose not to invest, they choose to spend. They may regret this decision later in life. The *be rich* will always live at least 15% below their income level. This magical 15% is invested so that it will increase their wealth pool, enabling them to do what they want later in life. This is why they invest.

Net Worth—A Good Way to Judge Wealth?

When we ask whether someone is a millionaire we are usually referring to their 'net worth'. That is, do they own a million dollars worth of things after you have subtracted all their debts? An average adult in our society might feel reassured when they calculate their own net worth. If they added the value of their house, their car, their television, stereo and so on, they might actually have a net worth of several hundred thousand dollars. They are rich! Or are they? Have a look at the money flow on the following page.

Figure 7.1 WEALTH MADE UP OF GOODS

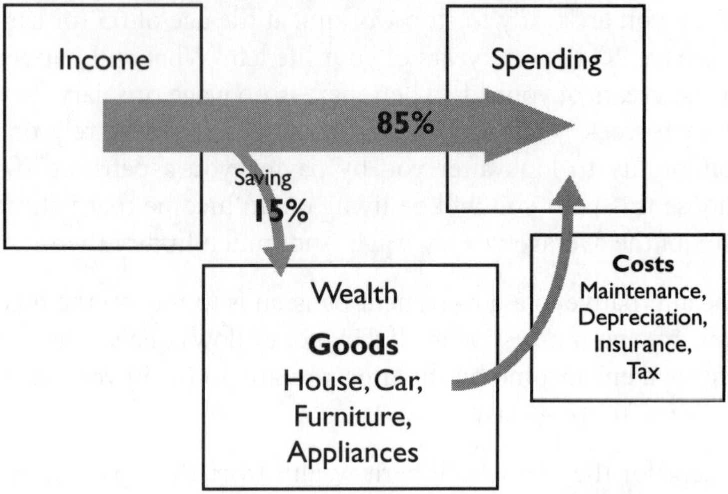

For You To Do...

Finding Your Net Worth

Take a walk through your bedroom and around the house. Look at your possessions and guess what you could get for them if you sold them today (that is, their market value, not their original purchase price).

Now complete the table opposite.

Two things stand out when you do this exercise. Firstly, most of what you own has probably gone down dramatically in value since you bought it. Secondly, many of your 'assets' are continuing to cost you money for cleaning, repairs and other expenses.

'Net worth' is a limited way of measuring wealth, and it can give you a false sense of security.

Assets (Items of Value)	Market Value
Clothing	
Shoes	
Furniture	
Sports equipment	
Electronic equipment	
Books, CDs, Videos	
Savings	
Other possessions	
TOTAL ASSETS (A)	
Liabilities (Debts)	Amount
Loans	
Credit cards	
Other debts	
TOTAL LIABILITIES (B)	
Net Worth	
Total assets (A)	
Total liabilities (B)	
NET WORTH (A – B)	

The *look rich* make two basic decisions that will keep them from becoming wealthy. Firstly, they spend most of their income on maintaining their lifestyle. This means that their wealth box does not grow as much as it could. Secondly, they mistakenly believe that their possessions (house, cars, boats, clothes) are what make them rich.

The problem with focusing on the 'goods' in the wealth box is that they do not produce any income. In fact, they are usually costing you money in repairs and maintenance. If you decided to retire tomorrow and live the rest of your life without your wage or salary, the 'goods' contents of your wealth box will not be of much use to you. That is the trap many *look rich* people fall into. They have spent their income on the outward appearances of wealth (the big house, the expensive car, the luxury holidays) but none of their 'goods' wealth will generate an income for them. Their house may be increasing in value, but so are all similar houses. The only way they can access this increased value is to trade down to a smaller house or a less desirable location.

A *be rich* person will also have a house, car, electrical appliances, clothes and so on in their wealth box, but in addition they will have 'investments'. Investments are what will produce an income for them. Their investments may include:

- Lending money to someone else and expecting them to pay interest for its use
- Buying property and renting it to others
- Buying a part of a company (shares) or owning a company, and receiving part (or all) of the profits.

When the income from investments is large enough to live on, the owner is financially free.

The different categories of wealth are shown in Figure 7.2. Notice the money flows. The 'goods' in the wealth box cost money, while the 'investments' produce money in the form of capital growth (things becoming more valuable) and/or income (interest, rents and dividends).

Figure 7.2
WEALTH MADE UP OF GOODS AND INVESTMENTS

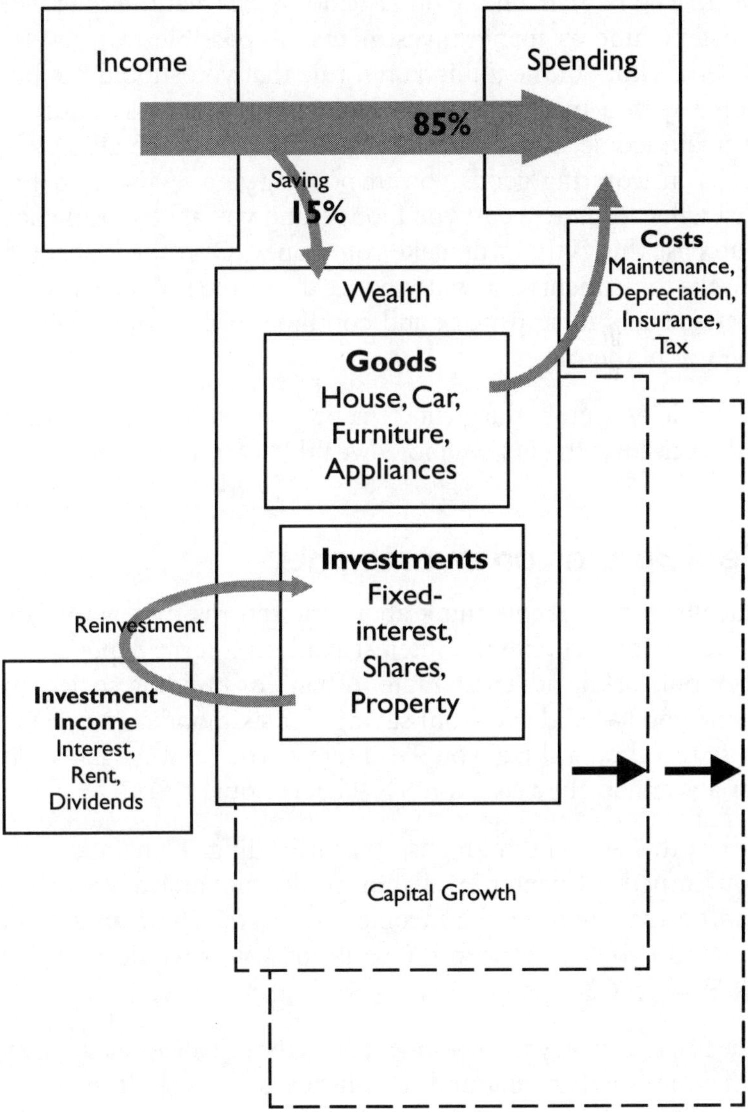

So you can see that net worth is a limited and misleading way to judge wealth. For the *look rich* their net worth is largely 'goods' that do not produce an income that would allow them to stop work. The *be rich*, on the other hand, know that their net worth must include as many 'investments' as possible to grow their wealth. Think of the millionaires' rule that you should not buy a home with a mortgage more than twice your gross household annual income. The reason for that should now be clear. If you focus on acquiring 'goods' you are pouring your savings into things that will continue to cost you money, and you are choosing not to purchase things that will make you money. Over the longer term, it is the investments that will produce the income which will enable their owners to stop work and continue to live comfortably for the rest of their lives.

As a rule of thumb, the greater the proportion of your wealth box that is in investments the more 'wealthy' you really are.

Real Returns on Investments

Usually, when people think about the returns they get on their money—for example the interest paid on a term deposit—they look only at the advertised rate. A bank or building society may invite you to hand over your savings for six months or a year and in return they will pay you 9% interest. You lend the bank $100 for a year and they give you $109 back. Sounds OK?

In fact this way of thinking is very misleading. Think about what you learned in Chapter 2; inflation erodes the value of your money and taxation reduces the income you make. The real return on the $100 you invest with the bank for a year would look more like Figure 7.3.

The real return on your investment has to be calculated after inflation has diminished its value and after the tax is deducted from income:

Real returns = Advertised rate – Inflation rate – Taxation

The inflation rate will vary from year to year and tax rates may change, but the principle is always the same.

Fig. 7.3 REAL RETURNS AFTER INFLATION AND TAX

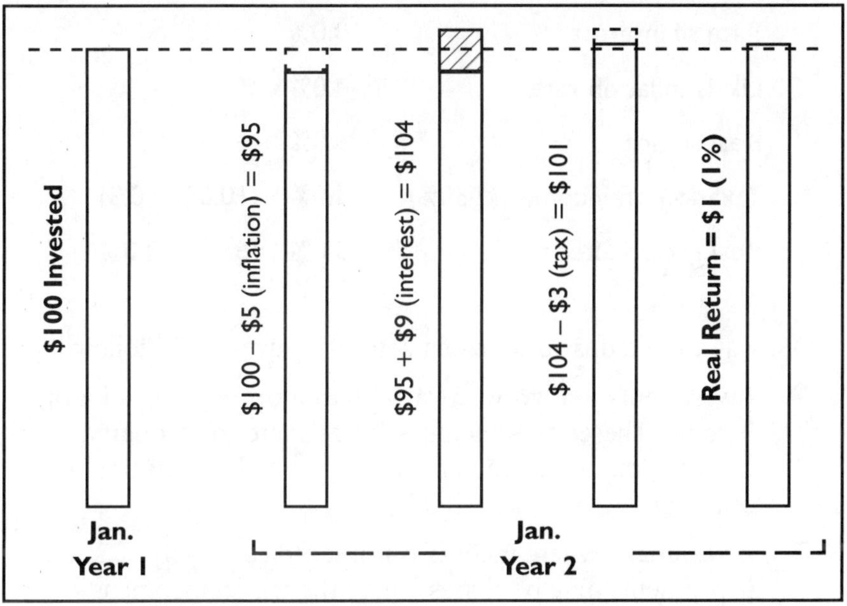

So What Does All This Mean For You and Me?

Firstly, it means that when we project into the future we have to be aware that the dollar amounts will not have the same value they have today. Inflation will have eroded the value of your investments. To get a more accurate idea of the future value of your investments you should deduct the inflation rate from the rate of return you expect from your investments. For example, if you expect to make a 10% return on your investments and you expect the inflation rate will be 4% over the long term, then your real return on the investment will be more like 6% (10% – 4% = 6%). Calculating this real return figure will give you an answer closer to today's dollar values.

Secondly, calculating real returns on investments can make you aware that you lose a part of your investment income in tax—the amount will depend on your marginal tax rate. Tax makes the picture even less rosy:

Rate of interest	10.0%	
Likely inflation rate	4.0%	
Real return	6.0%	
Taxation on income (@30%)	3.0%	(10.0% x 0.3)
Real return after tax	3.0%	(6.0% – 3.0%)

One way around this taxation of income is to invest in the following:

- Investments that grow in value without producing a lot of income. These investments, such as shares or property, have capital gains which are only taxed when you finally sell them.
- Investments where income is not taxed so heavily. These investments may be shares where the tax on income is already paid by the company and you gain imputation credits. They may also be investments in shares or property which are held in the relatively sheltered environment of your superannuation fund (see below).

Superannuation

In 1993 the government of Australia was so worried about the future of ordinary Australian working families that it set up a compulsory investment scheme. Instead of giving workers a pay rise, the government passed a law that employers should put the pay rise into a compulsory investment plan for an employee's retirement. The plan is known as the Superannuation Guarantee (SG) contribution. The amounts paid in by employers were small at first (3% of annual salary) but they have risen in steps. Employers will pay 9% of wages and salaries into superannuation by 2002.

For a person entering the workforce today it is estimated that they will need a lifetime accumulating 15% to 20% of their salary in superannuation to pay for a comfortable retirement. The 9% SG contribution from 2002 falls far short of this target. Some Australians are therefore not relying solely on the SG to fund their retirement; they have been making voluntary contributions to their superannuation fund for many years. This is their way of accumulating a wealth pool to support them in retirement.

Saving in a superannuation fund has pluses and minuses. The plus is that the tax on income earned by the fund is much lower than if you earned it directly—less tax means your wealth grows faster. The minus is that you can't get at your money until you are 55 years of age and retired, unless there are severe hardships or you are leaving the country permanently.

Superannuation is usually less attractive as a voluntary investment for younger people because you can't get at your money if an emergency arises. If you are just starting out on your working life you can pretend that the SG doesn't exist. You may be happy to allow the SG payments to accumulate quietly in a growth investment. You won't even know it is there because you never see the money. Meanwhile you can work at investing 15% of your income in a growth investment and start saving and investing your way to wealth.

Now that you have the overall picture, different types of investments will be dealt with in detail in the next chapters.

Chapter Summary

- Once you have started saving you then have to decide where to invest your money.
- Wealth can be measured by 'net worth', but this is a misleading measure.
- The part of your wealth which makes money for you is your investments.
- Returns on investments should be calculated after inflation and tax.
- Some of your investments may be in a superannuation scheme.

Chapter 8

Cash Investments

The simplest way to invest your savings is in 'debt' investments, where you lend your money to someone else and receive interest in return. In this chapter we will begin by looking at different types of bank accounts and then move on to debentures and bonds.

Cash Investments

Savings Accounts

Even if you are a teenager at school you have probably begun to use debt investments already. Your bank or credit union savings account is a debt investment. The idea is very basic: you own some money, you lend it to the bank for a while (until you decide how to invest it or spend it!) and they then return your money with an interest payment for allowing them to use it for a while.

Sounds simple, but of course it isn't. Inflation is eroding the value of your deposit, the bank and the government are charging fees and the interest rate on a savings account is so low that it's laughable. In the end you are probably going backwards as inflation and charges outstrip the interest gained, and this is without paying any tax. Savings accounts are not the way to grow rich. There has to be a better way.

Term Deposits and Cash Management Accounts

There is a better way, and you may have used this form of investment also. It's called a term deposit. Basically it is the same as a savings account except that you make a commitment to lend your money to the bank for a fixed period—one month, three months, six months, a year. This gives the bank some certainty and they are willing to pay you a higher rate of interest for this. You can withdraw your money early if you wish but there will be an interest penalty for doing so. The interest rate generally increases for the longer terms, and there is usually a minimum investment amount of around $500 to $1,000.

You may be earning 1% to 2% above inflation, and since there are no transactions there are fewer fees—you are gaining.

If you have a largish sum to invest, say $1,000 or more, you can open a cash management account. Here your money will be available any time, and it will also gain 1% to 2% above inflation.

However, sometimes it's hard to get excited about a 1% to 2% real gain. Some people look for more. This is where debentures and bonds come in.

Fixed-Interest Investments

Debentures and Bonds

Higher rates are possible by lending money to a company which wants to expand or to lend money to others. Lending to a company is called a debenture and usually attracts rates of about 3% to 5% above inflation. However, you are taking a risk if the company is not solid and prosperous. A safer place to lend at these interest rates is in government bonds.

From time to time the government (State and Federal) has to raise money to fund large projects such as building highways, airports and freeways. It asks the public to lend money and promises to pay it back in full at the end of three, five or ten years, along with a set rate of interest being paid to the lender every six months. The public lend their money to the government by buying bonds, which are a form of fixed-interest security.

Bonds can be bought directly from the issuer—for example the State or Federal Treasuries—or existing bonds can be bought from someone who already holds them and wants to sell. Existing bonds will need to be bought through a stockbroker and there will be a charge for the service.

There are also bond funds you can invest in. Bond funds are where a fund manager trades in bonds using the money of many investors. By buying and selling at the opportune time the fund manager hopes to make money for the unitholders of the fund.

Bonds seem to lock up your money for many years but there is an active bond market where you can sell your bonds before the due date if you need to get at your money urgently. There is a catch however. The government has promised to repay you the full sum (say $1,000) that you lent to it at the end of the term of the bond—perhaps after ten years. It will keep this promise and return your money ($1,000) after using it for ten years. No-one else has made that promise, so if you want to sell your bonds early you have no guarantee that a buyer will pay you the full face value.

For example, if you bought ten-year bonds with an interest rate of 6% five years ago, they still have five years to go until maturity when the government will repay the money. Suppose that since you bought your bonds five years ago the interest rate has gone up to 8%. This means that new bonds are now producing more income than your older bonds. If you try to sell your older bonds a buyer might only offer you a reduced price for them because they don't produce as much income as the newer bonds on the market.

A ten-year bond does not mean that your money is locked away for the full ten years. However, early sale may not get the full amount back for you.

Safety

Savings accounts, term deposits, cash management accounts, debentures and bonds are all ways you can lend your money to somebody else and gain interest payments for doing so. The income is predictable because you have entered an arrangement to lend your money at a certain price.

Although most people would regard cash investments as safe, there have been some spectacular crashes where companies and financial institutions have been unable to return all of their depositors' money. In the late '80s finance company Estate Mortgage and the Pyramid Credit Union closed their doors, leaving many of their depositors with large losses. These days banking regulations are tighter and the Reserve Bank will not allow any bank to fold—the same cannot be said for non-bank institutions.

In general, you should be cautious about any institution that is offering rates of return that are well above the norm for this type of investment. If they offer you, the depositor, a high rate of interest, they are probably charging a higher than normal interest rate on their loans to others. Why would someone borrow at a higher than normal rate of interest unless they had been knocked back by the cheaper bank lenders, possible because they were a poor risk and the bank was afraid of losing its money?

Returns

Even though cash and fixed-interest securities are generally safe and predictable, they have one serious drawback—they don't usually earn very high real returns. There are two reasons for this, which are looked at on the following page.

The Effect of Inflation

Firstly, inflation is continually eating away the value of the amount you have invested. The rates of interest are usually in the range of 1% to 4% above inflation, so real growth in your wealth is very slow.

The Effect of Taxation

The second reason is more important. A high proportion of wage earners are in the $20,000 to $50,000 income bracket. This means that every new dollar earned by these people is taxed at 30%. This is their marginal tax rate. An average worker who earns a dollar of interest from a cash or fixed-interest security will therefore have to pay 30¢ (30% of $1.00) in tax. So instead of thinking of the interest after inflation as being 1% to 4% we have to deduct 30% tax in order to get the real return.

People who want to grow their wealth are aware of these two limitations—low real earnings and taxed income—and they look for investments that have fewer drawbacks. There have been occasions when interest rates were high and fixed-interest investments did well. However, fixed-interest investments have never outperformed other investment types over a 20-year period. This means that if Mary held her money in bonds and Jane held her money in shares or property, after 20 years (any 20-year period you would like to nominate) Jane would always be in front.

You generally won't achieve high returns when you place your money in a bank account. Cash or fixed-interest investments are most suitable as short-term holding places on the journey to wealth. They are suitable places to accumulate savings for the purchase of an item, or to park money while deciding what to do in the stock market or in some other form of investment. Bonds can be a part of a person's total wealth pool because bond values tend to go up and down at different times compared to property and shares. However, cash investments are rarely the place where people try to grow their wealth pool in the longer term.

Chapter Summary

- You generally won't achieve high returns when you place your money in a bank account.
- Cash or fixed-interest investments are most suitable as short-term holding places on the journey to wealth.
- Even though cash and fixed-interest securities are generally safe and predictable they don't usually earn very high real returns due to inflation and taxation.

Chapter 9

Investing in Shares

During the last decade Australia has experienced its longest share boom in history. The sharemarket is mentioned in every television news bulletin and about half of Australia's adult population have become investors in shares.

The History

Shares have a long history. When European nations of the fourteenth and fifteenth centuries were exploring the world, enterprising individuals equipped ships to sail off to new lands to bring back stocks of spices, silks and precious metals. The organisers often raised the money for the voyage by selling shares in the cargo they hoped to bring back. Nobody could be sure that the voyage would be profitable until the ships returned to their home port a year or so later. In the meantime owners of the shares could trade them for money. If you felt that the ship had sunk, you tried to sell your shares. If you felt confident in the sturdiness of the ship and the skill of its crew you might buy shares from others. The place where the shares in the stock (cargo on the ship) were bought and sold became known as the stock market.

Today we still trade in the shares of an enterprise, but instead of a ship full of silks and spices, the enterprise may be a large bank, a car manufacturer, a chain of supermarkets or a mining company. Like the little ships of 500 years ago, the enterprise may profit or it may lose all.

When you buy shares in a company you are attempting to predict the future—you believe that the company will grow and prosper. Some fortunate investors believed in an unknown automobile manufacturer named Henry Ford in 1906, others believed in a mining company named Poseidon which fizzled out and disappeared with investors' money during the 1970s nickel boom.

Where do Shares Come From?

Shares come about when someone decides to sell part of a company to the public. Imagine Tina and Bill starting a company which produces pet food. They start small, with themselves and a few employees. Over the years the company grows and eventually Tina and Bill are the owners of T&B Pet Foods, a sizeable company worth $12 million. Tina and Bill know that they will need a lot of money to buy new buildings and machinery if they are to fulfil their dream of expanding into Asian markets and competing with the big pet food producers. They don't have that kind of money themselves so they go to the public and offer a part ownership in T&B Pet Foods.

What they do is organise to list T&B Pet Foods on the stock exchange, with 24 million shares worth $1.00 each. They would keep 12 million shares for themselves, because the company they built up is worth $12 million. The other 12 million shares are for sale. If investors think that the company has a bright future they will buy the shares. If there are more buyers than there are shares available, the price may rise as investors bid higher and higher prices for a share in a company with a good future. At the end of the first week the shares may be worth $1.20 each. If investors are not so sure of the company's prospects they may only offer 95¢ for each share.

At the end of the financial year T&B Pet Foods (now called T&B Pet Foods *Ltd*) may have made a profit. Before going public and listing on the stock exchange, all the profits would have gone to Tina and Bill. Now there are 12 million other shares and the shareholders receive a share in the profits. Shareholders will receive a dividend for every share they hold in the company.

The shareholders in T&B Pet Foods Ltd have two sources of wealth:

1. The income from their share of the profits, i.e. the dividends.
2. The increase in value of each share, i.e. the capital growth.

Do All Shares Grow in Value?

Over the past 50 years the average capital gain (increase in share price) of all shares listed on the Australian Stock Exchange has been about 7.0% per year and the average dividend yield has been about 3.3% per year. This means that an average return on shares is around 10% to 11% per year and is made up of an increase in share value and a share in the profits. Between 1945 and 1997 the rolling 10-year average return from Australian shares has been between 5% and 8% after inflation. In the 15 years 1983 to 1997 the return averaged 16.7% while inflation averaged 4.7% in that period.

Some companies have been spectacularly successful at what they do, and they have grown very rapidly. Most people have heard of Microsoft, the company which produces many of the programs which operate personal computers. With this type of company the dividend yield has been strong, but the capital growth has been enormous. Don't you wish you had been around to buy shares in the Ford Motor Company, Coca Cola, McDonald's or Microsoft when they were first listed on the stock market?

On the other hand, there are companies where the management has not been as good, or the product has not excited consumers, so the company has declined, resulting in dividends being low and the value of shares declining. Growth is not inevitable for any company.

This means that when you purchase a share in a company you are taking a risk. If the company does well you will be rewarded by healthy dividends and a rising share price. If the company does badly you may lose some or all of your money.

Figure 9.1 is a chart of Biota Holdings.

Figure 9.1
SHARE PRICE MOVEMENTS OF INDIVIDUAL COMPANIES

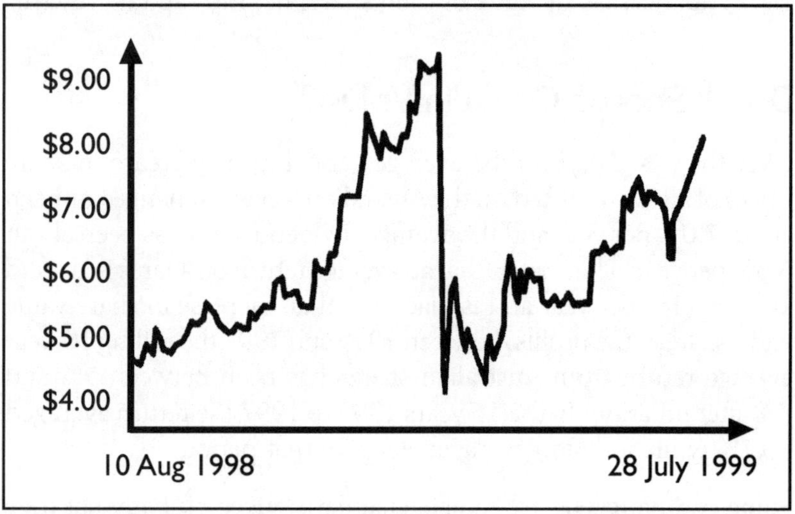

Biota Holdings is an Australian company that developed an anti-influenza drug, Relenza. In late 1998 there were hopes that the US authorities would approve the drug for general release. They did not. In mid-1999 those hopes were revived and investors thought that the company had a profitable future. By December 2000, Biota was back at $3.60. This shows you how volatile a share can be.

Types of Shares

Companies listed on the stock market come in all shapes and sizes. They are often divided into two main categories—industrials and resources, with industrials being the larger of the two. Industrial stocks include banks, telecommunications, retail, construction, tourism and transport companies, while the resources stocks include mining, energy (oil, gas, coal), minerals and gold companies.

Blue Chips

You may have heard the term 'blue chip' applied to some stocks. There is no single definition of a blue chip share but generally it means a share in a large company which has produced good dividends and respectable capital growth over a long period of time. Blue chip shares are generally regarded as less volatile and safer than other shares, but there is no guarantee that a large and profitable company will continue to be that way forever. Perhaps there was once a blue chip known as Smith's Horse Buggy Makers. Times change and management doesn't always make wise decisions, so the fortunes of a company can decline. There are no certainties on the stock market.

The Old and the New Economy Stocks

Recently there has been a tendency to refer to companies as belonging to either the 'new economy' of telecommunications, technology and the Internet, or the 'old economy', meaning everything else. This division can be misleading because many of the so-called old economy companies such as the banks are making a great deal of use of new technology in their business activities. Large retail companies are also establishing Internet retailing as part of their business.

Keeping Track of Shares

Shares are traded every working day on the stock exchange. These days the scenes of frantic young men waving bits of paper and yelling orders have been replaced by men and women in front of computer screens talking into telephones. Share trading is now computerised. A seller of 100 shares of T&B Pet Foods Ltd is computer matched with a buyer of 100 shares of T&B Pet Foods Ltd and the transaction is completed by a few keystrokes.

Because most shares are traded easily and frequently, their price is constantly fluctuating. If a company issues a poor profit report many people will sell their shares and look for a more profitable place to invest their money. As more and more people sell the stock the price tends to fall. The opposite happens if there is good news. People rush to buy the shares and the price rises. These daily movements can be followed in the business pages of the newspaper. On a typical day the sharemarket pages of *The Australian* look like Figure 9.2. The terms are defined opposite.

Figure 9.2 STOCK MARKET REPORT

Industrial Shares

Code	Stock	4pm Close	Move	Vol 100's	Buy	Sell	Year High	Year Low	Div Yield	P.E. Ratio
	A									
6016	AEGrowth units...	.45			.45	.55	.50	.34½		4.5
7378	AP Eagers.........	3.90	+.20	35	3.72	3.90	4.50	3.56	6.67F	18.6
9630	opt03...............	.25		66	.24	.30	.70	.21		
7137	A.G.L.	11.70	-.15	5469	11.70	11.75	13.02	7.63	4.36P	8.7
8848	ADV Group.........	.10			.08½	.10	.61½	.08½		
7856	AHC Ltd	.49			.30	.47	.68	.36	3.19F	14.2
8182	AHospCare.........	1.36		1544	1.36	1.37	1.40	.44½	1.65F	
7533	AI Eng..............	.13½	+.00½	385	.13½	.14	.73	.10½		12.9
7549	AJ Group stpld ...	1.15	-.01	12667	1.15	1.16	1.22	1.00	9.13	
7604	AJIndTru units	1.46	-.01	11005	1.46	1.47	1.512	1.30	8.97	
9818	AJLucas	1.59	+.01	20	1.58	1.69	2.02	1.01	4.09F	12.2
7335	AMP	19.31	-.329	45614	19.30	19.35	20.58	13.58	2.28	42.2
6316	AMPDiver units ...	2.42	-.06	3498	2.40	2.44	2.49	2.10	7.81	12.2
7044	AMPGrp FS insec	92.30	+.05	22	92.20	92.30	95.70	86.00	8.27	
8718	AMP IndTr..........	.95		7654	.94	.98	1.06	.93	9.89	10.2
9383	ctg	.30				.25	.30	.30		
8212	AMPOffice units ..	1.20	-.02	14706	1.20	1.21	1.25	1.02	7.10	13.3
7255	AMP Shop..........	1.36	-.02	2940	1.34	1.38	1.45	1.28	3.68	17.8
7136	ANZ.................	14.60	-.241	36595	14.60	14.68	15.41	9.73	4.38F	13.7
7844	AOG	1.70		77	1.70	1.72	1.90	1.106		
7857	AOL.................	.052	-.003	6385	.051	.052	.58	.02½		
7866	opt01	.01			.008	.013	.41	.007		
8603	AP Timber..........	1.63	-.02	753	1.63	1.65	3.55	1.55	2.45F	4.6
7845	APNewsMed	4.14	-.06	551	4.14	4.18	5.30	3.25	3.36F	21.2
8036	APS Chem	.37	-.01	387	.37	.38	.82	.37	16.22F	9.0
7478	ARB Corp	7.85	-.06	1	7.85	7.90	8.00	4.90	2.80F	17.2
8663	ASX.................	13.40	-.08	3547	13.38	13.40	15.491	9.66	4.19F	25.2
7847	ASandstne	.10	+.02	400	.07½	.10	.116	.06		4.5
7138	AUI..................	3.37			3.37	3.44	3.50	3.05	3.71F	41.2
8073	AVJenings	.48			.48	.51	.57	.39	17.86	2.7
8387	AXA Asia...........	2.93	-.09	13021	2.92	2.95	3.16	2.133	3.24P	13.8
8388	AXAAus PT units.	1.17	-.03	3260	1.17	1.19	1.25	1.02	7.47	13.3
7879	Abigroup	1.92	+.03	53	1.85	1.92	2.38	1.50	7.81F	6.3

© *The Australian* 9 January 2001

The Terms Used in the Stock Market Summary

Stock: An abbreviated name for the company.

4 p.m. close: The final price for the shares at the end of the previous day's trading.

Move: Any change in the share price since the previous day's close.

Volume: The number of shares that changed hands the previous day.

Buy: The highest final price being offered by buyers.

Sell: The lowest final price being accepted by sellers.

Year high/low: The highest and lowest price the share has sold at during the previous 52 weeks.

Dividend yield: The income given to shareholders from the company's profits for the year. It is expressed as a percentage of the share price. The letter 'F' means franked, or tax paid by the company, so the shareholder may have no further tax to pay on the income.

P/E Ratio: The price-earnings (P/E) ratio is a comparison between the current price of the share and the earnings or dividends produced by the share. This is a measure of how 'expensive' the share is because the P/E ratio tells you how many years' earnings it would take to buy the share. The P/E ratio can help an investor see whether a share is under- or over-priced compared to similar companies.

Summarising Market Movements

The All Ordinaries Index is one of the ways the Australian Stock Exchange (ASX) summarises the daily buying and selling on the stock market. The All Ords now represents 500 commonly-traded companies on the exchange. Other summary figures are the ASX200, the All Industrials Index and the All Resources Index.

The All Ordinaries Index, in one form or another, has been used to summarise trading on the Australian stock market since the late 1870s. The chart below shows the movement of the All Ords since then.

Figure 9.3 ALL ORDINARIES INDEX SINCE 1880

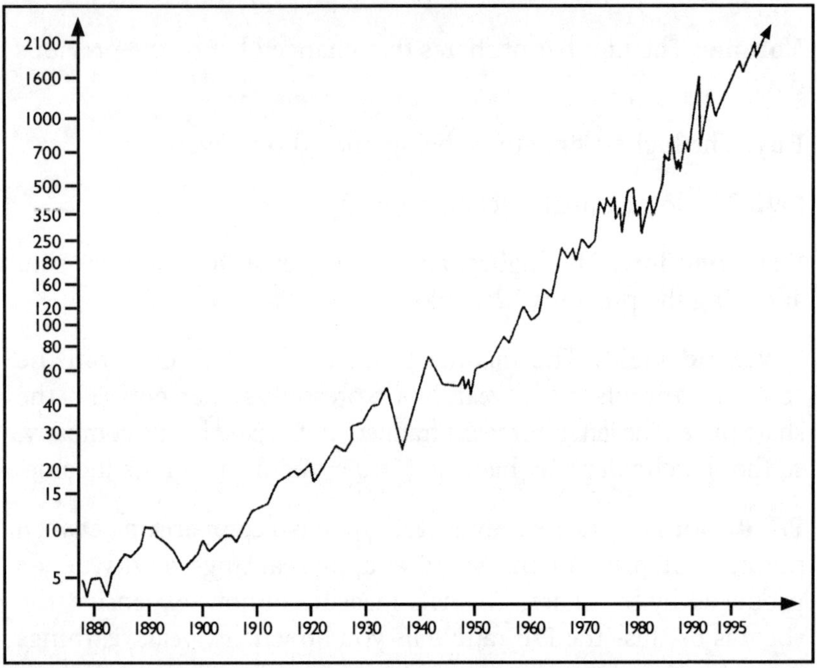

Other countries have their own summary indices. The publishers of *The Wall Street Journal*, Dow Jones and Co., decided last century that they would select 30 stocks to give a measure of how the market was behaving. The Dow Jones Industrial Average is widely quoted but it represents only a small fraction of the 7,000 stocks traded in America. A much more representative picture of stock market activity can be gained from the credit rating agency Standard & Poor's, who produce the S&P500, or better still, the Wilshire 5000, which despite the name, represents nearly 7,000 stocks. Perhaps we will hear more of the Wilshire 5000 in years to come.

There are also specialised indices for different types of companies. Nasdaq is an acronym for National Association of Security Dealers Automated Quotation. There are over 5,000 stocks listed on the Nasdaq exchange. In recent years the Nasdaq Index has become a measure of how well the new economy technology, telecommunications and Internet stocks have been selling.

In Japan the summary index is the Nikkei, in Hong Kong it is the Hang Seng. The index most often quoted for the London stock market is the FTSE100, which is short for Financial Times Stock Exchange 100 (FTSE is sometimes pronounced "foot-see").

The Advantages of Shares

For many cautious investors shares seem dangerously volatile. They find themselves torn between the apparent safety of cash investments and the promise of higher returns on shares. Which is the better way to go?

Shares Have Higher Average Returns

There are times, often after a market downturn, when shares do not do as well as cash investments. Over the longer term, however, shares tend to outperform cash and fixed-interest investments. The following table compares inflation, cash investments and share investments each decade from 1930 to 1995.

Table 9.1 AVERAGE RETURNS ON INVESTMENT TYPES

Period	Inflation %	Cash % returns	Shares % returns
1930–39	-0.7	2.2	10.2
1940–49	4.7	1.3	9.1
1950–59	6.0	1.4	10.8
1960–69	2.3	3.2	10.2
1970–79	10.4	9.0	5.9
1980–89	8.5	15.1	15.6
1990–95	2.6	8.2	10.3

Averages for a whole investment type can be deceptive. Some companies perform poorly, so they pay lower than average dividends and their share price (and your money) declines. Other companies do better than average in both dividends and capital growth.

The second way in which averages are deceptive is that they hide the ups and downs of the whole stock market. There are times when the economy is doing well—most people are employed and have money to spend, so business prospers and share prices rise. There are other times when things are not going well. People are unemployed or feel that their job is uncertain so they reduce their spending—companies sell less, profits are down and share prices drop. At times these drops in the share price are spectacular. The consolation is that there has never been a time when the sharemarket has not recovered from a drop and gone on to a new high (see Figure 9.4 opposite for some examples).

Each graph on the left-hand side of Figure 9.4 shows what happened to $100,000 worth of shares during a major stock market downturn. The corresponding graph on the right-hand side shows what happened in the longer term. Investors only lost money in each major market downturn if they had to sell their shares before the prices recovered.

If you can't afford to sit out a downturn and wait for the prices to recover, you shouldn't be in the stock market. Shares are only for investors with a long time horizon—at least five to seven years. If you need your money earlier than that you may find that you have to sell during a downturn in prices. Sometimes people panic when there is a market downturn and try to sell their shares. This can lead to substantial losses.

The lesson to be learned is—don't panic when the headlines scream "Blood Bath on Wall St" or something similar. Their job is to startle people into buying newspapers. Your focus is long-term wealth growth.

Figure 9.4 SHORT TERM AND LONG TERM

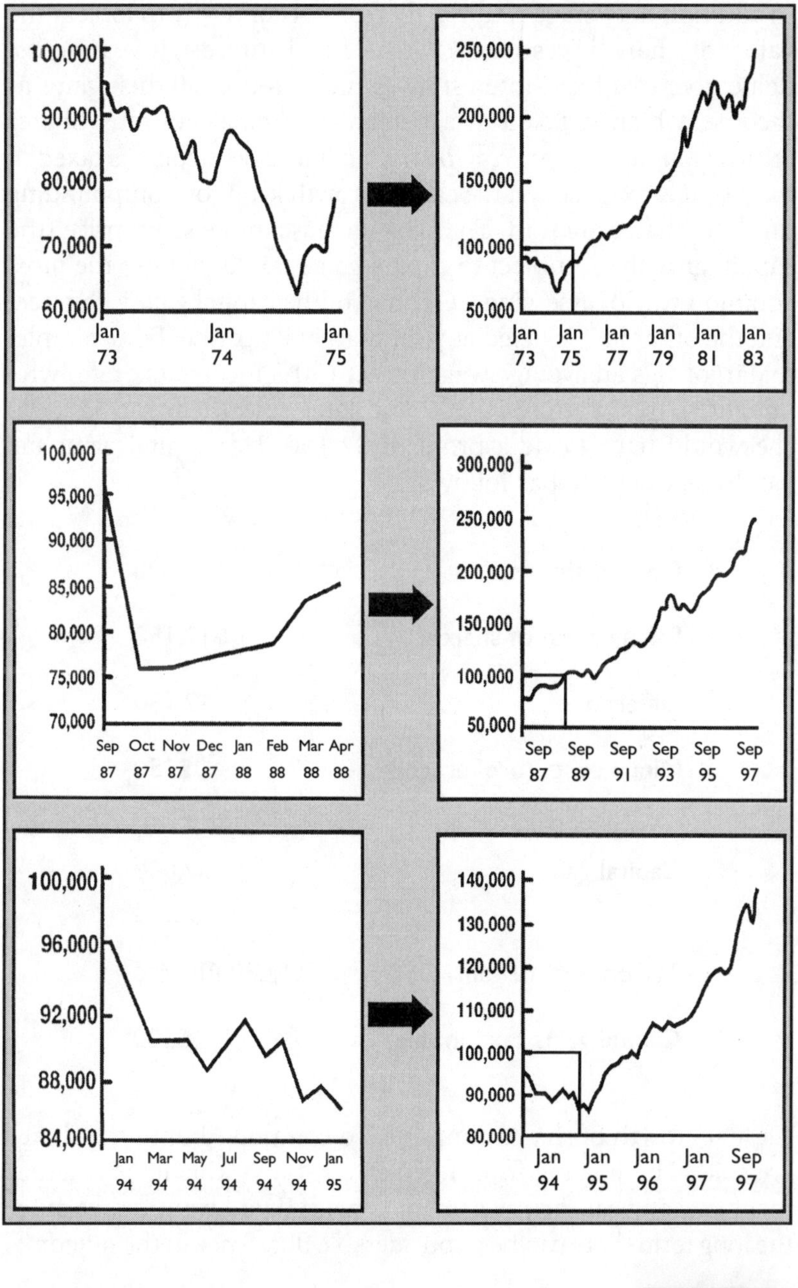

Shares Provide Capital Growth and Income

In addition to average returns, there is a second way to look at the value of share investment versus fixed-interest investments. Remember that fixed-interest investments return all their gains as *income*, which is taxed at a person's marginal tax rate. Shares return gains as *capital growth* and *income*. The income is taxed in the year it is received but the capital growth keeps on compounding until the shares are sold. Then the increase in the share price (the capital growth) is subject to capital gains tax. If you use the most common way of assessing CGT, half of the capital gain is tax free, and the other half is taxed at your marginal tax rate. For example, if Margot was an average wage earner (30% income tax rate) who bought shares worth $10,000 and later sold them for $12,150 she would have made a profit of $2,150. Her capital gains tax would be calculated as follows:

Cost of shares	$10,000
Selling price of shares	$12,150
Difference	$2,150
Minus costs (brokerage)	$150
Capital gain	$2,000
Tax on 50% of gain	$1,000 @ 30%
Capital gains tax payable	$300

Capital growth of shares continues to compound until the shares are sold. The income from fixed-interest investments is taxed as income each year the investment is held. If you want to invest for the long term there can be a considerable difference in the outcome.

Figure 9.5 shows the progress of the same investment amount in a fixed-interest investment (bonds) or a capital growth investment (shares). The rate of return is the same for the two investments, however each year the fixed-interest investment income is cut by taxation before it can be reinvested.

Figure 9.5 CAPITAL GROWTH VERSUS INCOME

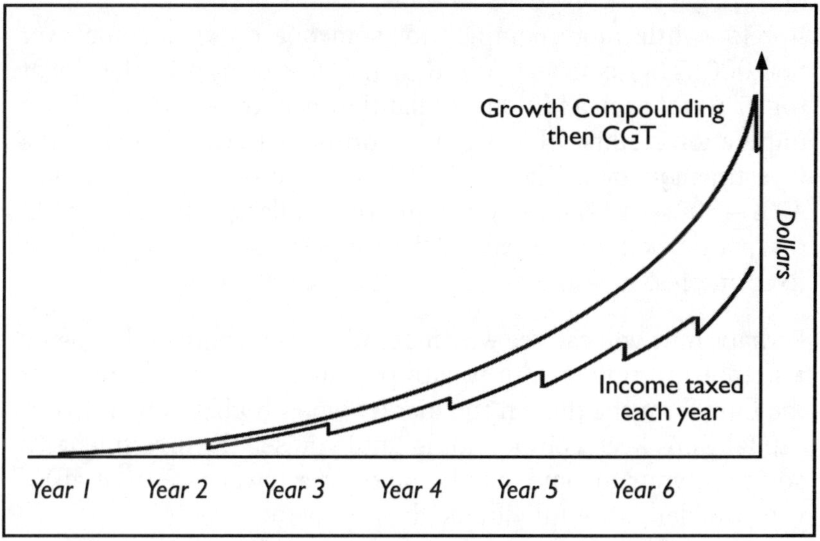

Share Income May Already Have Tax Paid

There is another reason why shares tend to be better than fixed-interest investments. Companies pay tax to the government on their profits. It would be unfair if the shareholder was taxed again on these same profits when they are distributed as dividends. The dividends therefore come to the shareholder with what are called 'imputation credits'. The government has given the shareholder credit for the tax already paid by the company. Any dividend which carries imputation credits is known as a franked dividend. Some newspaper share tables show franked dividends by placing an 'F' after the dividend yield figure.

The company tax rate from July 2001 is 30%, so companies will pay tax of 30% on their profits. What is left over is distributed to shareholders as franked dividends. An average worker would normally pay 30% income tax on this investment income. If the company has paid 30% tax and the shareholder would normally only be charged 30% tax on income, then there is no more tax to pay. Some people refer to these as 'tax-free' dividends, but it would be more accurate to refer to them as 'tax paid'.

It gets a little more complex for someone on an income over $60,000. This person is taxed at the rate of 47¢ in the dollar (or 47%) for each additional dollar they gain over $60,000. Their imputation credits will pay only a portion of the tax owing on the investment income. They will still have to make up the difference: 47% – 30% = 17%, or pay 17¢ in every dollar of dividends. Still, that's a lot better than paying the full 47% tax on income from fixed-interest investments.

Perhaps now you can see why most advisers recommend growing a sizeable portion of your wealth pool as shares. If you are in for the long term the dips in the market won't bother you and your capital gains keep compounding until you sell the investment. In addition, your income may be taxed at a lower rate (if at all) if your dividends are fully franked.

As a matter of interest, a recent survey by Access Economics showed that Australians differed in who had their wealth in direct share ownership. This is shown in the following table.

Table 9.2 SHARE OWNERSHIP BY WEALTH

	% Wealth			
	Bottom 50%	Top 50%	Top 10%	Top 1%
Superannuation	58%	22%	15%	5%
Shares	2%	15%	27%	61%

Buying Shares

You can either buy shares directly or indirectly. We will look at these two options individually.

Buying Direct

If you choose to buy directly you can purchase shares directly from the company when it first goes public and lists on the stock exchange (this is called a 'float'). When shares in a company are initially offered to the public you have to make an application on a special form. This form, called a prospectus, explains the company and its hopes for the future.

Many Australians have bought shares in companies which were sold by the government—Commonwealth Bank, Telstra and Qantas are examples. Initial listings are a good way to purchase shares if the company is sound and profitable. In this case the share price rises as investors try to accumulate more of the shares. In the late 1990s and early 2000s Internet companies (or 'dot-coms', after the Internet addresses ending in '.com') were highly favoured. Many investors rushed into the floats in the hope of rapid rises in share prices. April 2000 saw a major correction in the technology stocks, with some shares losing up to 70% of their value. It remains to be seen which companies will survive the shake out and go on to be prosperous enterprises.

Brokers

By far the most common way of buying shares directly is to buy into companies which have been on the stock exchange for some time. To do this you will need to go through a broker. Brokers differ in the services they provide and the prices they charge for completing a purchase or sale for you. Some brokers specialise in large transactions while others handle small purchases. The most expensive brokers, known as 'full-service brokers', offer background research on the company you are thinking of buying and will advise you on the wisdom of your choice. An alternative is a 'discount' broker who can arrange a purchase at a lower price but will not offer research advice on the company you are thinking of buying. The least expensive brokers are the Internet brokers such as Commonwealth Securities (www.comsec.com.au) or Sanford securities (www.sanford.com.au). With Internet brokers you can buy and sell for as little as $15 plus stamp duty.

Marketable Parcels

Just in case you get the urge to go out and purchase $20 worth of shares, you need to be aware of minimum marketable parcels. Whether you are dealing with a full-service broker, a discount broker or an Internet broker you will have to buy a minimum parcel of shares for your initial order. The size of the marketable parcel depends on the value of each share. After your initial order, though, you can buy and sell as many shares as you wish.

Table 9.3 MARKETABLE PARCELS

Share price range	*Marketable parcels*
0.5¢ to 25¢	2,000 shares
26¢ to 50¢	1,000 shares
51¢ to $1.00	500 shares
$1.01 to $10.00	100 shares
$10.01 to $50.00	50 shares
Over $50.00	10 shares

The other factor to take into account is the cost of brokerage as a proportion of your purchase. If you purchase $100 worth of shares, the cheapest Internet broker will charge you $15, or 15% of your capital (on top of this there is stamp duty to pay the government). The same $15 charge on a purchase worth $1,000 represents only 1.5% of your capital. The moral is, buying and selling eats into your profit, especially if you are buying and selling small parcels.

Indirect Share Ownership

If you have only a limited amount of money you may find that you are putting all you eggs in one basket if you buy directly into shares. Your savings may only allow you to buy a marketable parcel in one or two companies. An alternative approach is to pool your money with a large number of other people and have your risk spread over many different shares. This is a way of diversifying your risk. There are two ways you can own shares indirectly. You can buy shares in an investment company or you can enter a unit trust or managed fund.

Investment Companies

Listed investment companies such as Argo Investments Ltd or Australian Foundation Investment Company Ltd purchase shares in a wide variety of companies on the stock exchange. Investors then buy shares in the investment company and the price of the shares rises or falls depending on how the stock market sees the value of the investments owned by the company.

Managed Funds

Managed funds come in a bewildering variety. Some invest fund members' money in Australian shares, some in overseas shares, some specialise in Asian companies or South American companies while others focus on smaller companies that are likely to grow rapidly.

All fund managers charge for their services. There may be an entry fee and/or an exit fee, and there certainly will be an annual management fee. The annual management fee is referred to as the Management Expense Ratio, or MER. It is worthwhile comparing the MER for different funds you may be interested in investing with. The MER is a percentage of your total investment (not a percentage of the income the fund manages to earn!). So you pay an annual fee of 2% to 3% of your whole investment whether the fund is successful or not. The MER probably includes a 'trailing commission' or a small annual payment to the organisation that introduced you to the fund. This is one of the reasons that you can find fund analyses readily available on websites such as www.comsec.com.au. For example, if you purchase through Comsec the Commonwealth Bank will be paid a trailing commission of 0.35% each year your money is in the fund.

The funds that do a lot of buying and selling in order to get the biggest returns will usually be the ones that charge the highest annual fee. This could mean that you are paying a high annual fee for a lot of useless chopping and changing by the fund manager, or in the case of a good manager, you are paying for expertise in spotting undervalued companies and higher returns. When comparing the rates of return gained by different funds, you need to be aware that you are looking at past performance, which may not be repeated in the future. So look for funds which have been solid performers over a long period of time, not the one-year stars.

Index Funds

The cheapest fund type is the index fund. All the manager of the index fund does is ensure that the pool of investors' money is invested in a way that mirrors a particular index—the All Ordinaries or the Fifty Leaders for example. An index fund spreads your risk over many shares and doesn't charge an arm and a leg for doing so. There are often no entry or exit fees and the MER is very low. The drawback of an index fund is that it merely reflects the market.

More active fund managers try to select companies that will perform better than the market average. Unfortunately more than half of all fund managers fail to match the All Ordinaries, so you have to keep an eye on the progress of your fund to see if the fees are justified.

Between June 1995 and June 2000 the average retail equity manager earned 14.6% after fees, compared with 14.3% gain per year for the All Ordinaries Index. Funds rating agency ASSIRT concluded that only 5% of Australian equity fund managers demonstrated "skill beyond a reasonable doubt" rather than luck in outperforming the benchmark in the five years to March 2000! Surveys like this make it easy to understand why index funds are gaining in popularity among investors. Some financial writers have observed that index funds are not recommended to investors as often as you would expect simply because they do not pay a commission to the financial planner or organisation that recommends them.

Share Investing for Beginners

Investing in an index fund offers a good starting point for the beginner. You can begin with a fairly small amount of money but still spread your investment over a variety of shares. One example is State Trustees Premium Equity Fund, which invests in the ASX Fifty Leaders—the 50 largest companies listed on the Australian Stock Exchange. The minimum initial investment is $500 and you can add amounts over $300 at any time. There is a 1.50% entry fee and an annual fee of 0.85%. Vanguard Funds Management, the US managers who helped pioneer the idea of index funds, have several funds now operating in Australia. They have no entry fee but there is a 0.50% exit fee and 0.75% annual management fee. Unfortunately, their minimum initial investment is $5,000 which puts them beyond the reach of many beginner investors.

Managed funds are another good option for beginners. They often charge an entry fee of 2.0% to 2.5% of your investment. However, there are ways to avoid entry fees. There are discount brokerage firms—such as Personal Investment Direct Access or the Commonwealth bank's Comsec—that will supply you with the prospectuses for a range of funds. They will also rebate (return) to you most or all of the entry fee that is normally paid as a commission to a stockbroker or an financial adviser. With a little bit of care you can get started at minimum cost.

After the initial investment you can then sit back and wait for it to grow with compound interest, or you can save a regular amount into the fund. Remember the strategy of 'paying yourself first' that was mentioned in Chapter 5. Some investors use this strategy with a share fund. They arrange for their bank to automatically pay a monthly sum from their account into the share fund as an automatic savings scheme.

Dollar Cost Averaging

One interesting by-product of regularly saving into shares is *dollar cost averaging*. Ideally we would like to buy when the market is low and sell when it is high. This is very difficult to do—even the experts cannot tell you when a share price has peaked or bottomed out. What if there was a way of ensuring that you bought more shares when the price is down and fewer shares when the price is up? Well there is—it's called dollar cost averaging.

To keep things simple I will use an example of someone regularly buying quantities of a single share, rather than into a fund, but the principle works with either. Imagine you were investing $100 on the first day of every month. Over a period of 12 months you will have contributed $1,200. What happens if the share price falls during the year? The example in Table 9.4 shows a share price which falls then rises back to the starting point.

In Table 9.4 all that happened was that the share price fell then rose back to its original level of $1.00. Most uninformed investors would think that their investment had gone nowhere over the year. In reality, dollar cost averaging has led to a 20.8% return on their investment for the year.

Regularly investing into one single share does carry the risk that the company may fail. The company may be heading down the drain—with your money if you keep investing month after month. There is much less chance of pouring money into a failing company if your investment is spread over many different shares through an index or managed fund.

Table 9.4 DOLLAR COST AVERAGING

Month	Share price ($)	Number of shares bought	Total number of shares bought
January	1.00	100	100
February	0.95	105	205
March	0.90	111	316
April	0.85	118	434
May	0.80	125	559
June	0.75	133	692
July	0.70	143	835
August	0.80	125	960
September	0.85	118	1,078
October	0.90	111	1,189
November	0.95	105	1,294
December	1.00	100	1,394

Overall investment:	$1,200
Number of shares bought:	1,394
Value of shares in Jan. Year 2:	$1,394 + dividends (@ 4% = $55.76)
End of year total:	$1,449.76 for $1,200 invested
Return:	20.8% return on investment

A Radical Use of Dollar Cost Averaging

For a person in steady employment, with cash to spare, there is an even more radical approach to helping your investments grow. It combines dollar cost averaging with aggressive investment in the price slumps, and is called 'averaging down'. Once again, this strategy is safest for a fund (especially an index fund) rather than an individual company's shares.

It works like this. You decide to invest a set amount, say $100, on the first day of each month. So far it is just dollar cost averaging; if the unit price falls you end up buying more, if it rises you buy less. The new element is this: if the unit price drops by more than 10% from the previous purchase date you double your investment to $200 for the month. The choice of a 10% drop in price is quite arbitrary. A trigger of 10% is much less likely to occur than a drop of 5%, so you could adopt a 5% trigger if you had cash to spare and wanted to force yourself to invest more when the prices were cheaper.

If the unit price drops again by the first day of the following month by a *further* 10% below the last month's purchase price, you empty your piggy bank and scrape up enough to double last month's investment for the current month. This means that you are investing $400 now that the price has dropped in two lots of 10% from the start. You may even be able to cope with one more doubling if you have money lying about in a savings account and the unit price drops by a further 10% in the third month. Drops in unit prices of 30% or more would be a rare occurrence but you can see that the doubling of your investment in the dips would move the average cost for a unit down and it would significantly increase your returns.

For You To Do...

1. Construct your own table like Table 9.4 to see what happens:
   - In a year where the share price rises then falls to the starting point.
   - In a year when the share price keeps rising.
2. Recalculate the figures in Table 9.4 to see what would happen if you doubled your investment every month that the price dropped by 5% from the last purchase price.

   To do this you will need to redraw Table 9.4 using the existing figures for columns one and two. In columns three and four calculate the effect of doubling your previous investment ($100 to $200 to $400 to $800) each time the price drops 5% below the price for the previous month.

Chapter Summary

- Over the long term shares outperform fixed-interest securities.
- Shares return capital growth which compounds until the investment is sold.
- Shares also return income as dividends, some or all of which may be franked and therefore tax free for the average wage earner.
- The daily price of a share can be found in the stock market pages of newspapers.
- Shares are only for investors with a long time horizon —at least five to seven years. If you need your money earlier than that you may find that you have to sell during a downturn in prices.
- Share prices fluctuate because of either the wider economy or the progress of an individual company.
- Sometimes the whole stock market has a downturn; in the past it has always recovered and gone to new highs.
- The average price movements on the stock markets around the world are reported in indices such as the All Ordinaries, the Dow, the Nasdaq and the Nikkei.
- Shares can also be bought by combining your money with many other people in a listed investment company or managed fund.
- 'Paying yourself first' by making regular contributions to a managed fund is a good way for a beginner to get into the stock market.
- Regular share purchases make use of 'dollar cost averaging' which ensures that more shares are bought when they are cheap and less are bought when they are expensive.

Chapter 10

Investing in Property

In the previous chapter you learned that shares in a company are an equity investment because they give you ownership of something. As a part-owner you are entitled to a share of the income from the company (its profits) and a share of any increase in value of the company (its capital growth).

A second class of investment which fits into the equity or ownership category is property. Most people think of houses when you mention property, but property also includes:

- **Residential property:** houses, flats, units, town houses.
- **Commercial property:** office buildings.
- **Retail property:** shops—from corner milk bars to giant shopping centres.
- **Industrial property:** factories.
- **Tourism property:** hotels, motels, resorts.

Like shares, property investments can have an income component and a growth component. The income comes from rent paid by the tenants of the property, while the capital growth comes from the increase in value of the property as the location becomes more sought after.

Property Versus Shares

Although shares and property are both equity investments, there are several important differences between them:

1. Property feels permanent. There is something tangible about bricks and mortar that attracts some people. Unless you buy land on the edge of a cliff or beside a raging river, it will still be there in 50 years time. You can even stroll past your investment and have a look at how it is going. Shares are not permanent because the company you part-own may go broke and disappear.
2. Property is an even longer-term investment than shares. It will cost you between 5% and 8% of the property value and months of effort to get in and out of the investment. This is because you will have solicitor's fees, bank fees and stamp duty when you buy, and when you sell there will also be agent's and solicitor's fees. So when you buy property you do not approach the investment with the idea that you will give it a try and pull out after a year or so if you don't like it. Unless there are some extraordinary price rises in your area you are bound to lose money this way. With property you do your homework and thinking first, then you buy.
3. Property investment attracts some people because they have handyman (or woman) skills that they can use to increase the value of the property. This gives them a kind of control over the value of their investment that shareholders do not have. The flip-side of this is the fact that property investments need to be maintained. The roof may spring a leak, the hot water service may break down, the plumbing may become blocked. If you can fix these yourself you can save a lot of the costs of the property and increase your income.
4. Property is not a liquid investment. This means that it cannot be easily turned into cash in an emergency. If you decide to cash in your investment you will have to

advertise for a month or more, go through a sale or auction process and then wait up to three months until the money is handed over. You are also compelled to sell the whole property to get at some of the cash—you can't just sell off the spare room. With shares you can sell off a small parcel at any time you like.

5. The value of a property is much more difficult to establish compared with shares. You may get estimates from valuers or real estate agents in the area but these are at best educated guesses based on the prices paid for similar properties in the neighbourhood. No two properties are identical—the design, the decor, the garden, the outlook, the traffic noise and a dozen other factors make your property different from the others for sale. In reality you will only know the value of your investment when someone else hands over the cash after its sale.

   There is another reason why property is more difficult to value. A common indicator of property values is the median price paid for houses for sale in the city or suburb. The median (or middle of the range) price tends to rise for three reasons:

   a) People try to add value by renovating.

   b) Inflation is increasing all house prices.

   c) In some suburbs old houses are demolished and new expensive houses replace them, while in new suburbs the newer houses may be more expensive than the older ones.

   These three factors lead to a rise in median house prices, but this rise is only a statistic and, like all statistics, it can be misleading.

6. The final way in which property differs from shares as an investment is that property often needs a continued flow of cash to maintain and manage it. Management and maintenance for a residential property may cost around 25% of the annual rents.

What are the Returns on Property Investment?

This is a difficult question to answer because of the many different types of property. As a generalisation, residential property has long-term real (after inflation) returns of 1% to 3%. Long-term real returns on commercial property are between 3% and 5%.

Just as the All Ordinaries conceals variations in the performance of different shares, property averages do the same. For instance, in Sydney between 1977 and 1996 the median house price increased, but the size of the increase depended on how close to the city centre the house was. Between 0 kilometres and 6 kilometres from the centre, prices increased 827% over the 20 years. Between 6 kilometres and 25 kilometres from the city centre the increase was 702%, while suburbs beyond 25 kilometres only increased in value by 428%.

House prices in Sydney have increased faster than the other state capitals. Melbourne and Brisbane come next, with Adelaide and Perth following, and Hobart is last with the lowest price increases. In some outlying rural areas there has been a drift of population to the cities, so there is less demand for housing and house prices have declined in real (after inflation) terms.

Understanding What Happens in Cities

The best property investments are those which have the greatest chance of capital gain, so property investors need to know a little about the geography and characteristics of cities.

Historical Change

Fifty years ago the inner suburbs of many Australian capital cities were old, working-class areas. The houses were small—often terrace houses—and they were sometimes over 100 years old. They provided housing for the workers who made their living in the industrial areas on the edge of the central business district.

Gradually, middle-class city workers saw the advantages of living in the inner suburbs, close to the jobs and lifestyle of the city centre. They began to buy inner suburban houses and renovate them. As houses were renovated the suburbs became more desirable and more middle-class home renovators moved in—they (the 'gentry') eventually pushed up prices and forced the working-class residents out to the middle and outer suburbs. The renovation of the inner suburbs by the middle classes has been called 'gentrification'.

Life Stages

Different types of housing are needed by different types of people. Young urban professionals often prefer the freedom of an apartment without the responsibility of garden maintenance. The flat/apartment/town house is more attractive if it is close to the job centre, often near the centre of the city.

People starting families often want to own a detached house in the suburbs. The number of people in the population who are entering the 25 to 45 home-making age group is important as it will influence the demand for, and therefore the price of, suburban houses. The number of families in the home-formation group is influenced by birth rates and immigration rates. A high proportion of migrants arriving in Australia go to Sydney or Melbourne, and this will help keep houses in these cities in high demand.

Within most cities there are two competing factors at work. There is a push outwards because that is where the land is cheaper, but there is also a pull inwards because the centre has many attractions such as jobs, entertainment, theatres, nightclubs, and generally better access to all other parts of the metropolitan area (see Figure 10.1, overleaf).

An Ageing Population

In the first and second decades of this new century Australia is entering a period where a huge wave of people born after World War II—people known as the 'baby boomers'—will be moving out of the child-rearing phase of their lives. This bulge in the population may find the pull factors towards the city centre to be stronger than the push factors towards the city edge. As the baby boomers age they will continue—and probably speed up—the process of 'gentrification' in the inner suburbs.

Fig. 10.1 LIFE STAGES & PUSH AND PULL FACTORS

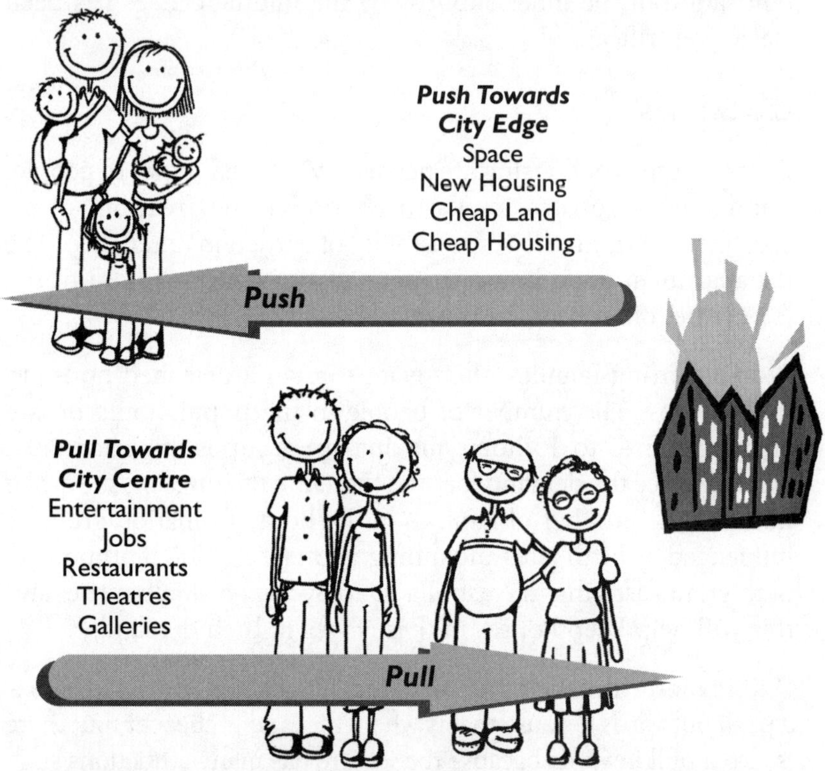

Choosing the Right Property

With these changes taking place in all cities, the property that is likely to show the most capital gain over the next 20 years is probably:

- Close to the city centre (within ten kilometres in large cities).
- Where gentrification has already begun or is likely to begin because adjoining areas have become gentrified.

- Aesthetically pleasing—an area with trees is more pleasant than an open area, hilly is more pleasant than flat.
- Unique or has rare characteristics—is beside a river, has historic buildings, is near a university, is on the harbour.
- Close to services such as shops, public transport, restaurants, banks, entertainment.

Location, Location, Location?

A final factor to consider when buying property is—are you buying just for location? Real estate agents are often quoted as saying that the three rules of property investment are "location, location, location". There is a certain truth in this—but it is a limited truth. Over the years there have been a lot of people burned by assuming that location was the only factor to consider. During the 1970s there was an apartment boom on the Gold Coast in Queensland. The locations seemed ideal. The only trouble was, too many apartments were built and there was a glut on the market. Many new owners found that they could only sell their apartments if they were willing to take a substantial cut in the price. That is the trouble with flats or apartments; someone can build 100 new apartments on your doorstep and your expensive investment flat is no longer a scarce commodity.

At present there are many town houses being built in inner areas of capital cities. This may lead to a similar glut on the market and a drop in prices so that investors lose money.

Another way to think about a residential real estate investment is that the building will depreciate, but if the land it is situated on is a scarce commodity (in a good location, near services, etc.) then you are more likely to receive a capital gain from your investment. For this reason I prefer a house and land to a flat or apartment because the land content is so much greater in the house and land compared to the flat.

So, for residential property, you might consider the amount of land you are buying in the right location, rather than location alone.

Buying Property as an Investment

Very few beginner investors buy vacant land as an investment for the simple reason that it returns little or no income. The only gain to be made is capital gain. There are considerable costs involved in buying and selling, as well as the costs of holding the land, such as loan interest, rates and maintenance. Something very dramatic would have to happen to your land or to the neighbourhood for you to make a decent profit.

Some investors buy commercial or retail property—office space or shops. This requires a lot of knowledge of the state of business in the area and an awareness of the plans of the large retail chains, who might build a new shopping centre a few blocks from your investment shop!

Most property investors buy what they are familiar with themselves—a residential property. This may be an investment flat, a unit, a town house or a house. Remember the land content factor. A house on a large block *in the right location* will always have scarcity value—they simply aren't making any more land in that area.

So how do you buy a house as an investment property?

Unlike shares, where you can start with $1,000 in a share fund, you will probably need other people's money to buy an investment property (see following chapter), so the place to start is with the lenders. The banks and credit unions lend for investment property and so do non-bank lenders such as Aussie Home Loans. A quick search on the Internet will tell you who has the lowest rates.

Most lenders will lend you up to 80% of the value of the property. The 80% level is their safeguard. If you fail to repay the loan they will take your property and sell it to get their money back. They know that even the most hurried sale will get them 80% of the value of the property—and all their money back. Some financial institutions will be prepared to lend you 90% of the property value if you take out mortgage insurance which will protect *them* (not you) from loss in case of a forced sale.

So where does the other 10% to 20% come from? It can come from two places. Either you have saved up the money or you can provide the financial institution with some other form of guarantee. The first, saving, is easy to understand and we have already looked at this in Part One.

The second method is looked at below.

Buying an Investment Property Using Home Equity

To understand some of the issues involved in purchasing an investment property we can follow a mythical couple named Nick and Gemma. The couple are both 30 years of age, so they have not yet accumulated a large wealth pool. They have been paying off the loan on their own home as quickly as they can. Now the house is worth $125,000 and they still owe the bank $55,000 on the mortgage. This means that they own $70,000 worth of their home. They could use this $70,000 of ownership (equity) as security on an investment property loan.

Let's say that they carefully search the market and compare the different houses for sale over a period of time. They eventually find a property that really seems to have potential for good rental income and sound capital growth over the long term. The property costs $130,000 and there will be bank costs, solicitor's fees and stamp duty of $5,000. The total cost will be $135,000.

The bank is willing to lend them 80% of the value of the home, which is $104,000. However, Nick and Gemma may offer the bank a second mortgage over their own home and use their $70,000 equity as security or guarantee for the remaining $31,000 ($104,000 + $31,000 = $135,000). The bank will look at the investment and loan package to see if the debt is less than 80% of the total value. Their calculations would look like Table 10.1 (overleaf).

The total for the remaining mortgage on their own home and the new investment loan comes to $190,000, which is 74.5% of the security being offered to the bank in the two houses. In this situation the bank would be willing to lend Nick and Gemma the full $135,000 needed to purchase the investment property and pay the costs. They wouldn't need any cash to make the purchase! If all goes well, Nick and Gemma will have two properties; their own home and the investment property growing in value for them.

Table 10.1 LOAN CALCULATION

	Value of properties	*Value of loans*
Own Home	$125,000	$55,000
Investment Prop.	$130,000	$135,000
Total	$255,000	$190,000
Loan Percentage		74.5%

The couple would have to be confident in their employment to undertake this commitment because if they can't maintain the repayments on the two loans the bank can sell both the investment property and their home to recover its money.

Now comes the balancing act. If all goes well, Nick and Gemma will find tenants for the investment property. This will provide them with rental income. On the other side of the accounts, they have to pay the bank interest on the loan, as well as paying a little bit of the loan money (called the principal) back each fortnight. The property will also have to be maintained, and if they hire an estate agent to manage the property there will also be management fees.

The cash flow is shown in Table 10.2 (opposite).

Notice that in the income column there are two items which will help Nick and Gemma afford to run their investment property—depreciation and a tax rebate. We will now look at these individually.

Table 10.2 **INCOME AND EXPENSES**

Income	*Expenses*
Rent	Agent's fees
Depreciation	Maintenance and repairs
Tax rebate	Rates

Depreciation

Firstly, what does 'depreciation' mean? It's easier to understand if you think of an industrial example. If a factory owner bought a new machine to make products, he has spent money in order to generate an income. Over time the machine will wear out, so that at the end of that time it is useless and has to be replaced. Each year of wear and tear on the machine is the cost the manufacturer pays to earn his income. The tax department applies the same logic to an investment property. The building was bought in order to gain a taxable income. The building (not the land) gradually wears out. This wear and tear is a cost incurred in earning an income. The investor is allowed to claim this cost at a rate of 2.5% of the building cost each year for 40 years.

There is only one catch. The 2.5% annual depreciation of residential buildings was only brought into law on 17 September 1987, and it applies only to construction after that time. Depreciation on residential buildings built between 17 July 1985 and 16 September 1987 is 4% per year for 20 years—so there are only a few more years of depreciation for these buildings. Any residential building built before 17 July 1985 does not come under the depreciation laws.

Details of the depreciation schedules on buildings are shown on the following page.

Table 10.3 **DEPRECIATION**

Residential Buildings		*Commercial Buildings*	
Before 17/7/85	0.0%	**Before 21/8/79**	0.0%
18/7/85 to 16/9/87	4.0%	**22/8/79 to 17/7/85**	2.5%
After 17/9/87	2.5%	**18/7/85 to 16/9/87**	4.0%
		After 17/9/87	2.5%

So why is depreciation important? Nick and Gemma can claim 2.5% of the construction cost of their investment property as an expense each year—without paying a single dollar out of their pockets. If the construction cost of the house was $65,000 when it was built, they can claim $1,625 (2.5% of $65,000) each year. This has the effect of reducing their taxable income, so they pay less tax.

Tax Rebate

The second income factor which will help the couple run their investment property is the tax arrangements. Nick and Gemma's cash flows can be seen in Figure 10.2 (opposite). Their income appears to go up as they receive rental income, then it drops as they pay out expenses. If their expenses are greater than their income from rent their overall taxable income is reduced and they get a partial (30%) tax rebate. The final cost to them is deceptive because the depreciation allowance on the building appears as a 'cost' but it really hasn't cost them anything.

If the costs (fees, interest, maintenance) of running the investment are less than the total rental income, the owners are making a profit on their investment. In this case the investment is 'positively geared'. If the costs are greater than the income and the owner is making a loss, the investment is 'negatively geared'. (See Chapter 11 for more information on gearing.)

Figure 10.2 CASH FLOWS ON A RENTAL PROPERTY

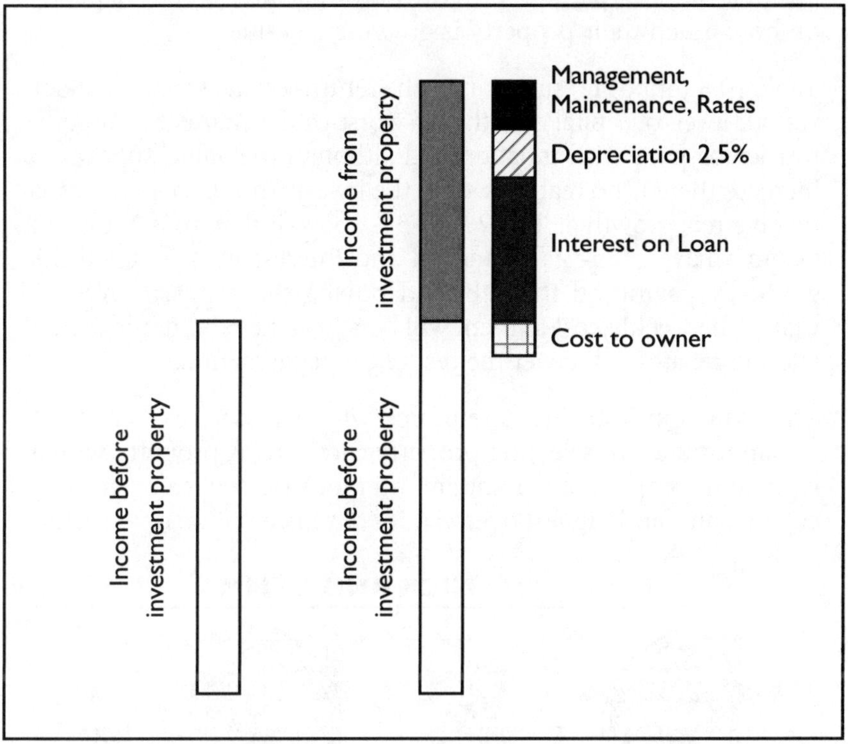

The cash flows in Figure 10.2 show that the rental income plus depreciation plus the tax rebate almost covers the cost of managing, maintaining and paying interest on the property—almost, but not quite. The couple will still be out of pocket to cover the gap each week.

One way of looking at the rate of return on the investment is to calculate the Internal Rate of Return (IRR). This is calculated by comparing the costs to the owners ($70 per week) with the overall growth on the value of their investment: the growth in its value (capital growth) plus the growth in the fraction they own through repaying the mortgage. The internal rate of return can be surprisingly high. This is because the owners are actually investing very little in the house each week or each year. For Nick and Gemma the internal rate of return on their investment depends on how much their property is growing in value.

Table 10.4 (opposite) summarises the returns on the property under various levels of capital growth. In a worst-case scenario the property just keeps pace with inflation and although the value appears to increase there is no real growth in the investment. Other scenarios involve real growth at 1%, 2% or 3% above inflation. If Nick and Gemma have a 25-year principal and interest loan they will be gradually paying off the debt and buying the property over 25 years. The weekly cost to them will be $70—the rent, depreciation and tax rebates will cover the rest of the repayment cost.

The figures in Table 10.4 reinforce what was said earlier about the importance of selecting property carefully. A property with a high land component in a sought-after location will show greatest capital gains and highest overall rates of return on the investment.

Figure 10.3 NICK AND GEMMA

Nick and Gemma and the bank buy an investment property

25 years later: Gemma and Nick own their own home and an investment property...or two...or three...

Table 10.4 RETURNS ON INVESTMENT PROPERTY

	INVESTMENT GROWTH RATE			
	Inflation + 0%	Inflation + 1%	Inflation + 2%	Inflation + 3%
Property value	$130,000	$130,000	$130,000	$130,000
Purchase costs	$5,000	$5,000	$5,000	$5,000
Loan	$135,000	$135,000	$135,000	$135,000
Capital growth	3%	4%	5%	6%
Inflation rate	3%	3%	3%	3%
Interest	8%	8%	8%	8%
Property expenses	23%	23%	23%	23%
Depreciation				
—buildings	2.50%	2.50%	2.50%	2.50%
—fittings over 5 yrs	$8,400	$8,400	$8,400	$8,400
Tax credit	31.50%	31.50%	31.50%	31.50%
After-tax cash flow	-$3,625	-$3,625	-$3,625	-$3,625
Cost per week	$70	$70	$70	$70
Internal Rate of Ret.	14.58%	24.89%	33.65%	41.34%
Pre-tax equivalent	21.28%	36.34%	49.12%	60.63%

Calculations assume Nick and Gemma are earning $38,000 and $15,000 per year respectively and the investment property is held in the name of the higher taxpayer.
It is important to note that the internal rate of return decreases in time, as the interest costs, depreciation on fittings and loan costs all decrease as deductions. However, the cost per week stays fairly static.

At the end of 25 years Nick and Gemma will own the property and it can continue to give them an income for the rest of their lives. Their overall cost will be how much they have had to support the investment each week for 25 years ($70 × 52 weeks × 25 years = $91,000). This may seem a lot for a house that was priced at $130,000 but inflation has been pushing up values and eroding the cost of their payments over the 25-year period. Even with no capital gain—the house just keeping pace with inflation—it will be valued at $272,191 by the end of the 25 years.

With capital gains of 1%, 2% or 3% above inflation their $91,000 investment will be worth considerably more—this is shown in Table 10.5.

Table 10.5 TOTAL VALUE AND FINAL PAYMENTS

	INVESTMENT GROWTH RATE			
	Inflation + 0%	Inflation + 1%	Inflation + 2%	Inflation + 3%
Value of property after 25 years	$272,191	$346,559	$440,226	$557,943
Total cost for owners over 25 years: $70 x 52 x 25	$91,000	$91,000	$91,000	$91,000
Value of investment after costs	$181,191	$255,559	$349,226	$466,943

Further Investing

If Nick and Gemma can pay off their home mortgage quickly they will have more and more equity in their home to support further borrowings. Also, without the mortgage payments, they will have the spare cash to support several more investment properties.

In time they can have a portfolio of properties quietly growing in value and being paid for (at least partially) by the tenants and the taxation office.

Listed Property Trusts

If buying, managing and maintaining an investment property is not for you, there is an alternative property investment—listed property trusts. Like share funds, property trusts pool the investments of a large number of small investors and use the money to buy office buildings, shopping centres, hotels and factories.

There are property trusts that specialise in different property types—commercial, retail, residential, industrial and tourism. Most of these funds are listed on the stock exchange and they tend to follow the general movements of the stock market.

Some are huge—the Westfield Trust has over $4.6 billion invested, General Property Trust has over $4.2 billion invested. On the other hand there are smaller trusts which have not yet accumulated large amounts of assets, such as MTM Entertainment Trust with $83 million invested, or Global Property Trust with $28 million invested. You can find out more about listed property trusts from online brokers.

Which property trust you choose will be influenced by whether you want income or capital growth. Remember that income, even if it is reinvested, will be taxed each year as you receive it. Growth will only be taxed as capital gain when you sell the investment. If you are focused on growing your wealth pool, growth-type investments are the way to go.

Different trust managers have different strategies to meet the needs of income seekers or growth seekers. Some managers will have a high growth/low income strategy, some will aim for balanced growth and income, while others will aim for low growth/high income. There are also split trusts where the investor can choose to buy income-oriented units or growth-oriented units.

Just as it is possible to invest in an index fund which tracks the average performance of the sharemarket, it is also possible to invest in a property index fund for a comparatively small amount of money. The State Trustees Premium Property Fund, for example, spreads investors' money over a range of property trusts and sets out to match the ASX Property Trust Accumulation Index. Initial investment is $500 and additions of $300 can be made. There is a 1.50% entry fee, no exit fees and annual fees of 0.88%. If you want to invest indirectly in property but don't know which fund to choose, an index fund may suit your needs.

As with share funds, a beginner investor can start small and gradually buy more units over time. However, all investors need to be prepared for rises and falls in the unit price. During an economic downturn there will not be the same high demand for factory space or hotel rooms or office buildings. Given time however, the economy will recover and demand will increase, causing prices to rise once more.

Remember, property investment is for the long haul.

Chapter Summary

- Property is an equity investment and can experience capital growth.
- Property is different to shares in a number of ways.
- Property can give good returns if it is selected wisely.
- When investing in residential property you should consider:
    - Wider changes in society which may influence demand.
    - The land component of an investment.
    - The probability of capital gains.
- Investors can buy property indirectly by investing in a listed property trust.
- Property index funds allow investors to spread their investment risk over many different funds.
- All property rises and falls in price as general economic conditions fluctuate.
- Property is a long-term investment.

Chapter 11

Other People's Money

So far the discussion of investment strategies has mostly focused on your own savings in the wealth pool and trying to grow this wealth. You know that equity investments generally produce a higher long-term return than income investments. You also know, from the earlier discussion on compound interest, that time is the key.

In the chapter on property another key element in wealth growth was introduced. In the example of Nick and Gemma investing in property, the couple were not only using their own wealth, they were using other people's money—the bank loan. Using other people's money for investment is called leveraging or gearing because both levers and gears magnify output compared with the input. For example, you could use a small force on the end of a crow bar (lever) to shift a rock you would not have been able to move alone. Similarly, if you own a bicycle you know that on straight level stretches you can arrange the gears so that one turn of the pedals produces several turns of the back wheel.

Figure 11.1 LEVERS AND GEARS

When you use other people's money you are doing much the same as a lever or a gear. You are turning a small force (your money) into a much larger force (the larger investment returns). You can see this in the example of the well in Figure 11.2. The water level in the well represents the starting point of your investments. Raising the bucket up the well is like having your investment grow. The rate of returns would be represented by how fast the handle is turned to raise the bucket. A low rate of return—such as on a term deposit—would mean a half a turn of the handle per year. A high rate of return, such as on a high-growth share investment, might mean two turns of the handle per year.

Figure 11.2
THE WELL WITH A SMALL WHEEL

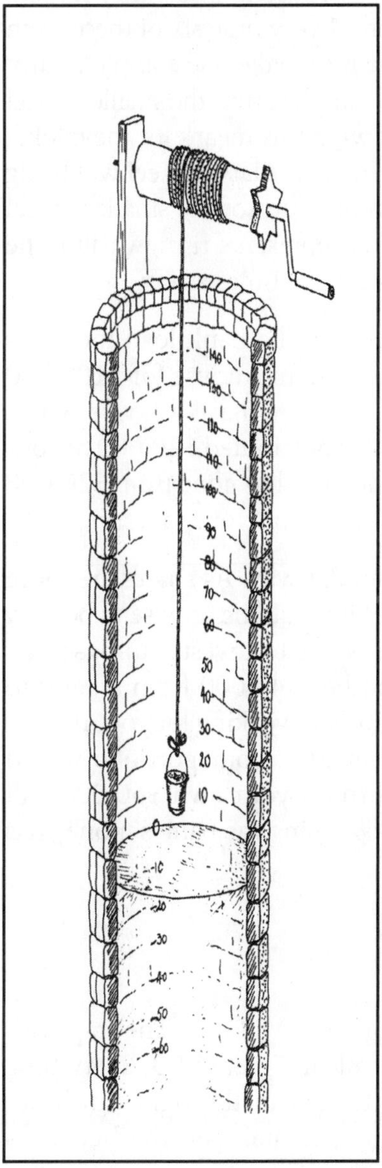

Figure 11.3
THE WELL WITH A LARGE GEAR

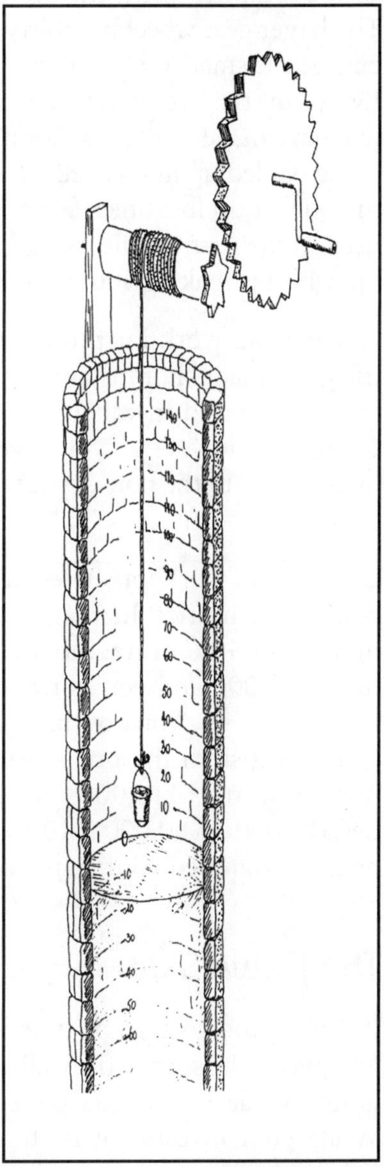

What would happen if some inventive person attached a much bigger gear wheel to the small wheel already on the well? Have a look at Figure 11.3. The gear wheel already on the well has only six teeth, so one complete turn brings the six teeth back to where they started. The larger gear wheel has thirty teeth. Every time six of these teeth engage the smaller wheel they cause it to make one complete turn. Every time the large wheel does one complete turn the smaller wheel will have made five turns. Think of what this means for the bucket being hauled up in the well. One turn of the large wheel will bring the bucket up five times faster than one turn of the smaller wheel used in the past. As the rising bucket represents rising wealth, the big wheel is making your wealth grow five times as fast.

Gearing can work for property because the bank loan increases the gains made. For instance, if you bought a house for $100,000 and it increased in value by 10% you now have a house worth $110,000. However, if you have only contributed $20,000 of your own money to the house, your ownership has gone from $20,000 to $30,000, which is a 33% gain for you on your investment.

Gearing can work for shares in a similar way. As shares are more volatile (their price fluctuates more) it would be unwise to borrow more than 40% of the money you want to invest. Suppose you have $60,000 and you borrow another $40,000 from a bank to invest in shares. You now have $100,000 working for you. If there is a 12% rise in the price of your shares, your portfolio would now be worth $112,000. The return on your own $60,000 will be: $12,000 ÷ $60,000 × 100 = 20%. Using the bank's money has greatly magnified your gains.

The Down Side

It sounds too good to be true doesn't it? Well it is. The trap with gearing can be seen in the well example in Figure 11.3. Everything is fine while the handle is being turned in the right direction. While your investment is showing a capital gain the bucket is rising rapidly up the well.

But consider what will happen when your investment suffers a capital loss. Suppose there are plans to build a freeway on the front doorstep of your rental property, or the sharemarket takes a 40% dive overnight. Suddenly the big gear wheel starts turning in the opposite direction and the bucket plummets down the well at an alarming speed. The bucket may even go down to the surface of the water (what you started investing with) and keep going so that you are losing your original investment money.

It would be a disaster if you had to sell your investment at that point. Fortunately, investors who buy wisely and gear sensibly will be able to sit out the downturns and wait for the property market or the stock market to come back up again.

Just as gearing can increase your profits, it can also increase your losses. Investors who have been most badly burned by gearing into shares are those who borrowed on a system called margin lending.

Margin Lending on Shares

With margin lending the investor borrows using the shares themselves as security. ('Security' means that the lender can take the asset if you fail to pay back the loan.) Careful lenders will want to be sure that they will get their money back, so they will usually lend only a limited percentage of the value of the security. With a house the lender will lend 80% to 90% of the value of the property as the house is unlikely to fall more than 20% in value. With an investment as volatile as shares, a lender such as a bank might have a rule that the loan must never be greater than 70% of the security (the shares).

Suppose an optimistic (or naïve or greedy or ignorant) investor, Kate, decides to gear heavily into the sharemarket during a boom period. She borrows $70,000 from the bank, combines it with $30,000 of her own money and purchases $100,000 worth of shares. If all goes well, the large bank loan will multiply her returns and make her rich quickly.

But what happens if the shares fall in value? Suppose there is a minor drop of 15% in the value of the shares. Kate's shares will now be worth only $85,000. The bank will get nervous because its loan is now more than the regulation 70% of the value of the security. Kate borrowed $70,000 but the bank will now only be happy if the loan is reduced to 70% of $85,000, which is $59,500. Kate will receive a 'margin call' demanding that she immediately repay $10,500 of the loan. Unfortunately for our investor, the only way to come up with the demanded $10,500 loan repayment is to sell some shares—at a loss now that the market has fallen 15%.

And it can get worse! What if there is a major correction and the market falls a further 20%? Now Kate is in real trouble. She will receive a margin call from the bank demanding loan repayments to bring the loan back to 70% of the new—much lower—share value. Having just sold shares at a loss to repay the first margin call for $10,500, she now has to sell more shares at an even greater loss to repay the bank another $11,900. Kate's sad position can be seen clearly in Table 11.1.

Table 11.1
DROPPING SHARE VALUES & MARGIN CALLS

Share price	*Value of shares*	*Loan amount (70% of value of shares)*	*Loan repayment needed to reduce loan to 70% of share value*	*Loan as % of share value after repayment*
	$100,000	$70,000	–	70%
15% drop	$85,000	$59,500	$10,500	70%
Further 20% drop	$68,000	$47,600	$11,900	70%

The lesson is simple. Don't be greedy, and select your investments carefully. This applies to all investments, but it is even more important when you are borrowing. If it is a property investment, select property that is unlikely to suffer a capital loss. If it is a share investment remember that share prices routinely fluctuate, sometimes by as much as 35% (or even more) in one year. If the stock market is reaching the top of a boom the following correction may be as great as 50% of the share's value. Highly speculative stocks can lose 90% of their value. Never put yourself in a position where you will have to sell in a downturn. If you decide to gear by means of margin lending (using the shares as security) then be very conservative and keep your borrowings below 30% to 40% of the share value.

Borrowing Against Home Equity

A safer way to borrow for share purchases is to use some other security which is less likely to fall in value. In the previous chapter Nick and Gemma borrowed using the equity (ownership) in their home as security for the loan. They could easily have done the same thing for share purchases. If the sharemarket declined the bank would not worry about the safety of their money since the house is still there in case of failure to repay the loan. In this situation Nick and Gemma could ride out any sharemarket downturn and wait for the economy to recover. They have not lost any of their investment until they sell—all their losses are only paper losses.

This highlights a useful strategy in growing your wealth pool—using the equity in your own home. Most Australians want to buy their own home to gain a sense of security and safety for themselves and their families. There are also financial advantages of buying your own home. Even though renting is cheaper in the short term, you do not end up with an asset which has grown in value while you were living in it. Furthermore, the capital gains on your own home are not taxed. Home ownership also has many psychological advantages. You know that no one can evict you, you can decorate it to your own personal tastes, you can even renovate in a way that suits you.

By paying off the mortgage (the bank loan) as quickly as you can you not only save huge amounts in interest but you gain an asset that can be used as security to gear further investments. Paying off the mortgage frees up income so that it can be used to support other investments. Some Australians know the value of saving interest by repaying the loan quickly, but very few know how to use their home equity to create a large pool of investments that will grow in value at a compound rate of interest.

What makes Nick and Gemma different to most of their neighbours is their willingness to use their home equity to gear into relatively low-risk investments. Taking this road to wealth meant that they had less income to spend for a while but they gained a sizeable asset in the long run.

A word of caution, however. Borrowing by using the family home as security should not be undertaken lightly. If the investment goes badly you not only stand to lose you investment capital but the bank may repossess and sell your home in order to recover its money. Speculative share investments or fancy tax minimisation schemes bought in this way come with a serious risk of taking with them both your capital and your home if they go south.

The Cost of Gearing

Gearing is borrowing, so there is interest to be paid and loan money to be repaid to the lender. Obviously you would follow the rules for all borrowing and search for the lowest interest rate available. How will you repay the loan?

Your investment should produce income such as rents or dividends. These can help you meet the interest and loan repayments. You can also claim all loan costs and interest costs as a tax deduction. This may lower your taxable income and result in a tax rebate—where the taxation department repays some of the tax that was taken out of your wages by your employer. With a property investment you can also claim a deduction for depreciation on the building if it was built at the right time (see Chapter 10).

If your investment has been bought for capital growth rather than income, it is unlikely that the income will cover all your costs. Where the cost of borrowing is greater than the income it produces you are said to be negatively gearing your investment. You would negatively gear investments so that you receive a tax rebate from the loss you are making, but the bottom line is that you will have to support your investment each month by putting some of your wages towards the loan repayments. This cost from your own pocket each month will depend on the dividend/rental income and the size of the tax rebate. Do some careful calculations before you commit yourself.

Chapter Summary

- Using borrowed money to buy investments is called leverage or gearing.
- Gearing increases the speed at which things happen:
  - Increases in wealth are faster.
  - Decreases in wealth are faster.
- Geared investments should be bought only after thorough homework.
- Margin loans, which use shares as their security, can cause severe capital losses in times of share price downturn.
- The family home can be used as security for low-risk geared investments, even if it is only partly paid off.
- Gearing often costs money because the income from a growth investment may not match the interest costs.

Chapter 12

Economic Cycles

In previous chapters there was some reference to shares or property going up or down in price over time. To understand why this happens you need to have some idea of how the economy works. You could spend years at University studying this topic—this short description is no more than a general introduction to the subject.

The economy tends to work in cycles. You can think of a 'cycle' as a circle where you will come back to the beginning if you set off around the circle. The face of a clock represents a cycle—the minute hand starts at the 12 and an hour later it comes back to the 12 position again. A 24-hour day is a cycle and a year is a cycle. No matter where you start on the cycle you will eventually arrive back at your starting point again.

Another way to think about a cycle is in the form of a wave, or lots of waves. With a series of waves you could start at a crest, go down into the trough, rise up the other side and you are back to a crest again. Then you could go down into the next trough, and so on.

Economic conditions tend to follow a cycle. At one time we may be up on a high with everything going well, then we decline into a low when everything economic seems to be going wrong. We eventually climb out of the low and head up towards a new high. This cycle is sometimes referred to as the 'boom–bust' cycle.

Figure 12.1 CYCLES

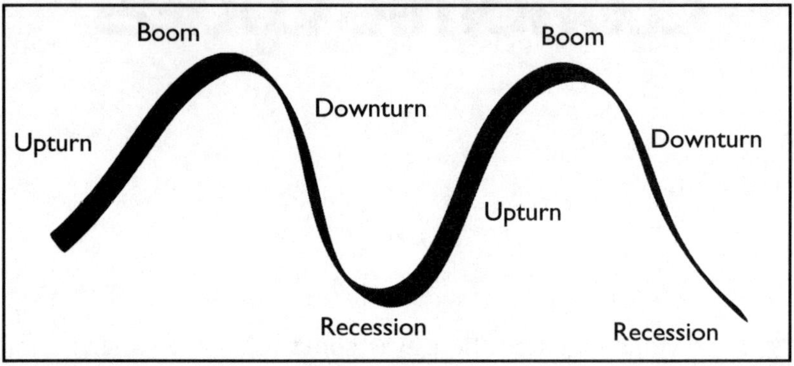

The Boom–Bust Cycle

Why does the boom–bust cycle happen? We know some of the reasons, but economists don't understand it well enough to be able to prevent it happening.

Following is a basic explanation of the boom–bust cycle.

1. Approaching the Boom

We can start looking at the cycle as it climbs towards the top—the boom. The amount of activity in the economy is increasing. There is more money available to borrow and interest rates are low, so borrowing is cheap. People borrow this cheap money to build homes for themselves and to buy cars, clothes, appliances and so on. Industries are profitable because people are buying more. They put on extra workers to cope with the demand and the unemployment rate falls. There is more demand by overseas countries for our commodities. Share prices near their peak.

2. The Boom

A falling unemployment rate increases people's confidence in the future so they spend more and save less. Industries produce more to meet the demand. People borrow for housing and investment and the sharemarket increases to record high prices as more investors flock into a booming market. Demand for goods and services is so high that scarcity causes price increases. Price increases lead to demands for wage increases, which lead to more price increases. As the prices of goods and services increase, the value of the dollar falls—we have inflation. The longer this goes on the worse the inflation gets.

3. The Downturn

Everyone becomes concerned that inflation will reduce the value of their savings. The government becomes concerned that the economy is 'overheating'—that is, growing too quickly. The government, through the Reserve Bank, decides to slow the growth in order to control inflation. One way to control price rises is to reduce the amount of spare cash people have in their pockets by raising interest rates. This means that home mortgages and credit card purchases are more expensive. Now that money costs more, people borrow less. There are fewer houses built and fewer shares bought. The enthusiastic greed of the rising sharemarket may suddenly be replaced by irrational fear as investors scramble to sell their shares while the prices are still high. The pessimists who believe that prices will fall are known as 'bears'. When there are more sellers than buyers the sharemarket is said to be in a 'bear market'. The sharemarket may suffer a sudden and large drop in value—a 'correction'. Money may move from the stock market into property, so the property boom may last longer than the stock market boom.

4. The Trip to the Bottom

Higher interest rates damp down demand and industries begin to lay off workers. People become anxious and more pessimistic about the future, so they spend less and save more. This reduces demand for goods and services even further, and more workers are sacked. Profits decline and returns from the sharemarket fall, leading to depressed share prices. Real estate prices fall from their peak. Lack of demand means prices no longer rise, and neither do wages, so inflation falls.

5. The Bottom

The economy has now slowed down. Inflation is under control but unemployment is up and people are fearful of spending. Share prices are at their lowest for some time because industries are not making very large profits. There may be business failures because it is very difficult for the sharemarket to attract investors' money. Investors have shifted their money into bonds and debentures in order to get higher returns. If the economy has actually shrunk in size for two three-month periods in a row it is called a 'recession'.

6. The Climb Up

The government is very unpopular at this stage. They have controlled inflation but they seem to have wrecked the economy in the process. Now that inflation is controlled the Reserve Bank of Australia can lower interest rates and increase the amount of money available to be borrowed. As interest rates come down people are more willing to borrow to build homes and to invest. Demand for goods and services increases and industries are more profitable. Money flows back to the stock market and share prices rise rapidly. The optimists who buy shares, believing that their value will increase, are referred to as 'bulls'. When the buyers outnumber the sellers we have a 'bull market'.

7. Approaching the New Boom

Demand for goods and services means more jobs. People become more optimistic and spend more, creating more demand and more jobs. Share prices reach new highs. Demand leads to scarcity, prices rise, inflation starts to creep up again—and the cycle continues.

The clock in Figure 12.2 is called an 'economic clock'. It is a common way of showing economic cycles.

Figure 12.2 **THE ECONOMIC CLOCK**

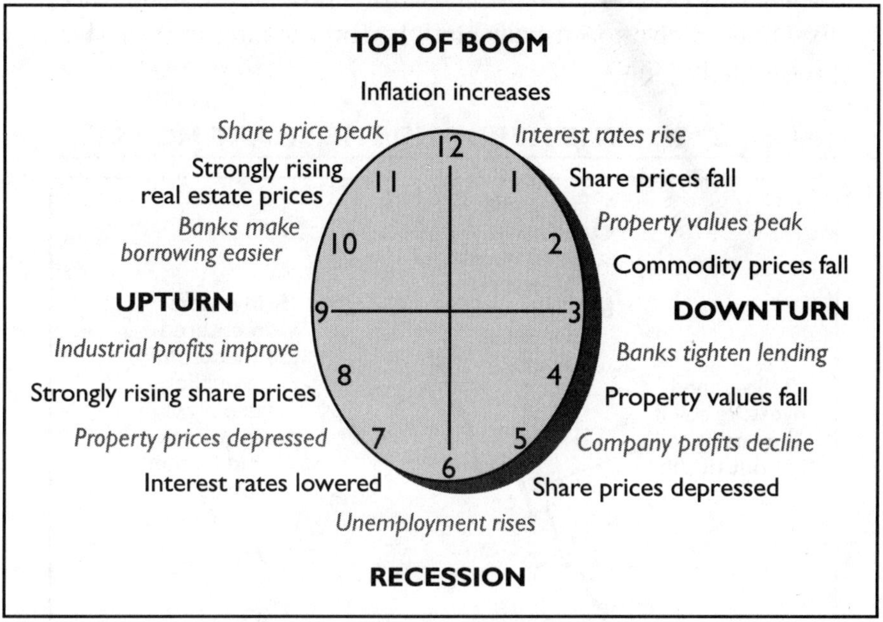

The Economic Cycle and Investments

A basic knowledge of economic cycles is useful for people wanting to grow their wealth because it helps them avoid buying into investments at the wrong time and selling at the wrong time. Now that you know about the basics of the economic cycle you can see that your returns on investments will be greatest if you buy when the prices are low and sell when the prices are high.

Economic Cycles and the Sharemarket

To be a share trader you need to know the economy and the market very well. In the first few months of 2000 Rupert Murdoch sold $180 million worth of shares in News Corporation, a company he controls, and moved the money into his family company. In mid-April 2000, the booming sharemarket suffered a major correction which was especially hard on technology/media stocks. Many people didn't time it so well.

Knowing the business cycle will help you to decide when to hold your savings as cash while you wait for a drop in the share price. Experienced investors usually buy when others don't and sell when others are buying.

Figure 12.3 THE HERD AND THE SMART MONEY

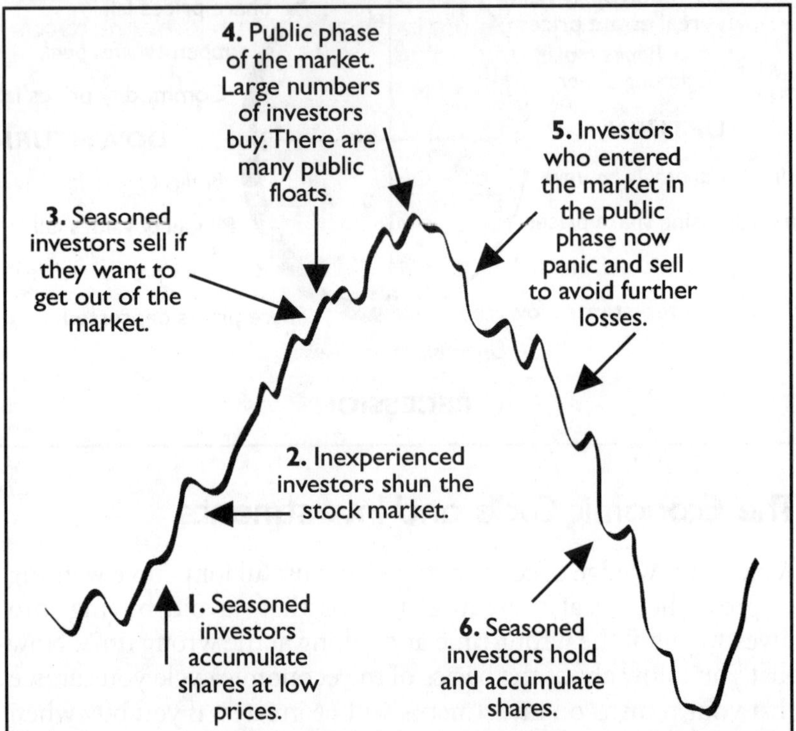

Figure 12.3 shows a simplified version of the boom–bust cycle in the stock market. Seasoned investors are those who understand about economic cycles. They buy more in the 'gloom' of a correction when the shares in solid companies are undervalued because of panic selling. Inexperienced investors do the opposite. When the prices in the market have fallen there are many stories of people who have lost money, so the inexperienced investors are fearful of investing and head for the safety of fixed-interest or cash investments.

When the recovery occurs, the seasoned investors enjoy the ride up as they watch their cheaply-acquired shares increase in value. By the time the inexperienced investors decide that it is safe to re-enter the market, most of the gains have occurred and they are buying at boom prices—often from the seasoned investors who have decided to cash-in their profits. The lesson is simple—buy in the gloom and sell in the boom. Or, if you are a long-term wealth accumulator, buy more in the gloom and less in the boom.

Time In and Timing

Some people are natural gamblers. They enjoy the thrill of the risk. If you are one of these people you can gamble at a casino or on the stock market. Chances are, you will not get rich doing so. To grow your wealth you need to be patient and allow compounding to work for you. There is a lot of evidence that hopping in and out of different shares will not produce the steady long-term gains you are after. As a general rule: *time in* the market is more important than *timing* the market.

This does not mean that you should ignore the time on the economic clock. You will make greater returns on your investments if you buy at the bottom of a cycle. If you buy at the top of the cycle you may have to wait for a year (or even years) before the share or property price rises again and you begin to make a capital gain on your investment.

Investment adviser Austin Donnelly has an interesting analysis of the impact of timing of share purchases. Using Australian stock market data for the past 40 years, he concluded that your chances of making a reasonable return on a share investment in the short term (five years) is significantly influenced by the timing of your purchase decision.

This makes sense when you consider two investors, one buying at the peak of a boom when prices are inflated, and the other buying in the gloom when prices are at their lowest. Returns over the next five years for the two investors will look very different. The peak buyer may see his or her share value drop and then rise to its original price, while the gloom buyer may see his or her share value climb steadily towards the next boom. The key to using this information is to know where you are in the economic cycle.

A summary of Austin Donnelly's analysis is shown below.

Table 12.1 THE BEST TIME TO BUY

Zone	*Average dividend yield**	*Probability of 8% or more capital gain in next five years*	*Description of the zone as a time to buy shares if you have a five-year timeframe*
5	9.59% to 5.50%	79%	Very favourable
4	5.48% to 4.69%	49%	Favourable
3	4.68% to 4.24%	32%	Medium to neutral
2	4.23% to 3.77%	43%	Unfavourable
1	3.76% to 2.49%	28%	Very unfavourable

* Published in each Friday's *Australian Financial Review*

Compiled from Austin Donnelly's *Sensible Share Investing 3rd Edition* (Wrightbooks, 1999)

Is Timing Important?

If you are an older investor who is placing a large proportion of your wealth in the stock market and you are relying on the price to stay up so that you have enough money to live on, timing is very important. Timing is also important if you are about to make a substantial investment—such as the money from a redundancy payment or the proceeds of a house sale. In these circumstances, if the timing indicators are unfavourable, it may be wiser to spread your investment over property, shares and fixed interest. You could ease your way into the stock market gradually over a year or two. That way you can even out the price fluctuations by dollar cost averaging.

If you are a young(ish) investor who is saving regularly into the market, timing is not as important. In this case dollar cost averaging and compounding will work in your favour over the longer term. If this is you, forget about 'get rich quick' and focus on 'get rich slow' by steadily accumulating investment wealth.

It's the Last Doubling That Counts

A final word on time. If you re-read the section on compound interest you will find that it is the last doubling of your investments that really counts. If your investments are growing at 7% per annum they are doubling every ten years. If you are investing for an early retirement, the last ten years before you retire will see your investments grow more than they have done for the entire period of your saving and investing before that.

This principle can be seen in a simple story: imagine there is a weed growing in a pond. The weed begins as a small patch in the middle but doubles in size each day. If the weed takes fifty days to cover the whole pond, on what day will it cover *half* of the pond? Since the weed doubles in one day, the answer must be the forty-ninth day.

Suppose you begin your investing at the age of 20 and plan to retire at the age of 60. All the hard work and investment growth in the 30 years up to age 50 will be surpassed by the growth (assuming a 7% return) that takes place in the ten years between 50 and 60. So, if you want to be a millionaire by the time you are 60, you will need to have accumulated $500,000 by the time you are 50.

The golden rule with all investing is

START NOW.

Index

I

J

L

M

T

U

W